Victorian Fiction Research Guides are issued by the Victorian Fiction Research Unit within the Department of English, The University of Queensland.

The Unit concentrates on minor or lesser-known writers active during the period from about 1860 to about 1910, and on fiction published in journals during the same period. Among the **Victorian Fiction Research Guides** currently in preparation are bibliographies of Ada Cambridge, 'Sydney Grier'[Hilda Gregg], and L T Meade.

We would be interested to hear from anyone working on bibliographies of these or other authors of the period, or on indexes to fiction in journals of the period. Any information about the locations of manuscripts, rare or unrecorded editions, and other material would be most welcome. Information about gaps or errors in our bibliographies and indexes would also be appreciated.

The subscription for the current (seventh) series of **Victorian Fiction Research Guides**, which commences with this volume, is $40 (Australian) for four **Guides**; single volumes $12. Copies of earlier Guides are available at the following prices: Series 1,2,3,4,5: $25 (single volumes $7); Series 6: $35 (single volumes $10).

Orders should be sent to Dr Barbara Garlick and editorial communications to the general editor, Professor Peter Edwards, both c/- Department of English, University of Queensland, Australia 4072, fax 7 3365 2799; email b.garlick@mailbox.uq.edu.au.

i

Bram Stoker
1906

BRAM STOKER
(Abraham Stoker)
1847-1912

A BIBLIOGRAPHY

Compiled by WILLIAM HUGHES

Victorian Fiction Research Guide 25

Victorian Fiction Research Unit
Department of English
The University of Queensland

ISBN 0 86776 641 7
ISSN 0158 3921

Published by
Department of English
The University of Queensland
Australia 4072

Contents

Cover of the first paperback edition of *Dracula*, 1901

Introduction

I

"Qui ne connaît *Dracula* aujourd hui?
Qui connaît son auteur, Bram Stoker?"[1]

The popular assumption that the figure of Bram Stoker has been eclipsed by the fame of his best-known fictional character has, to a certain extent, been generated by the specific needs of modern literary criticism. The author's life is for the most part obscured and becomes in a sense necessary only where it confirms the critic's theoretical point — that the text, for example, mobilises or expresses personal neuroses or sexual guilt.[2] Arguably, such critical exercises say more about the critic's own preoccupations and cultural background than they can ever say about those of the author. Equally, the critical attention devoted to *Dracula*, to the almost-total exclusion of the author's other writings, betrays not merely that text's status as a fruitful field for criticism, but acknowledges a popular interest in the *Dracula* myth which has been generated in part through cinematic adaptations which are at times only nominally based on Stoker's original plot.[3] The cultural concept of *Dracula* as novel and character, and the associated biographical construction of the author are thus rooted largely in a world that is both post-Freud and post-Lugosi.[4] To depart from this consensus, to view Stoker by way of Victorian and Edwardian documents and material culture, is to come face to face with the perverse realization that, in Stoker's lifetime at least, the creation was probably less well-known than the creator. Indeed, the question must be raised as to how much Stoker himself was regarded as an author rather than as a theatrical personality in his own lifetime.

*

Abraham Stoker junior was born at 15, The Crescent, Clontarf, County Dublin, on 8 November 1847. He was a sickly child, who, by his own admission, was not expected to live.[5] His father, Abraham senior, was a member of the British civil administration in Ireland, a clerk based in the Chief Secretary's Office of Dublin Castle. Mundane as this post may sound, he was confident enough to describe his profession as simply "Gentleman" when completing his son's baptismal certificate at the Anglican parish church of St. John the Baptist, Clontarf, on 3 December 1847.[6] Presumably because of his unspecified illness, Abraham junior was educated first at home, and subsequently at a small private day school run by the Reverend William Woods, a Protestant divine. From this basic information, and from the cultural development of education in the period, it may be deduced that the author's pre-university experience was one which schooled him in the discourses and social graces which linked the Anglicised, Irish Gentleman to his English counterpart — Protestantism, the Classics, and the physical culture of a generation influenced by Carlyle and Muscular Christianity.[7] It is also worth noting that, despite the financial difficulties that frequently beset large families, Stoker's brothers followed their father into respectable professional careers: William, George and Richard studied medicine; Tom joined the Indian Civil Service. Bram himself was called to the English Bar in 1890.

On 2 November 1864, at the age of sixteen, Stoker matriculated at Trinity College, Dublin. His college career does not appear to have been academically distinguished. Despite his later claim that he "had got Honours in pure Mathematics", his name does not appear amongst those who achieved the distinctions of Moderations or Respondency.[8] Stoker, still styled as Abraham, received the degree of Bachelor in Arts [sic] at the Spring Commencements on 1 March 1870, and was admitted to the degree of Master in Arts, as was customary at Trinity College, without further study on 9 February 1875.

The author did, however, distinguish himself in other areas of College life, advancing these achievements as integral, rather than supplementary, to the more formal requirements of his scholarly environment. The influence of Carlyle and Kingsley is apparent in the rhetoric of Stoker's own assessment of his university career:

> In my College days I had been Auditor of the Historical Society — a post which corresponds to the Presidency of the Union in Oxford or Cambridge — and had got medals, or certificates, for History, Composition and Oratory. I had been President of the Philosophical Society; had got Honours in pure mathematics. I had won numerous silver cups for races of various kinds. I had played for years in the University football team, where I had received the honour of a "cap"! I was physically immensely strong. In fact I feel justified in saying I represented in my own person something of that aim of university education *mens sana in corpore sano*.[9]

This phase of Stoker's life has again been the subject of comparatively little critical attention. Where modern scholarship does touch upon the author's College career, it is normally in connection with his defence of the poetry of Walt Whitman in the debating chamber.[10] An investigation of Stoker's involvement in the two College debating societies prior to and following his graduation in 1870, however, provides both a fascinating insight into the student preoccupations of the period, and a reminder again of the homosocial, gentlemen's club-like tenor of College life in the nineteenth century.

Written minutes for the Dublin University Philosophical Society are extant only from the 1867-8 session. These record that "Mr A. Stoker" read a paper entitled "Sensationalism; in Fiction and Society" at a general meeting held on 7 May 1868.[11] This paper, Stoker's first, with his subsequent addresses entitled "Shelley" and "The Means of Improvement in Composition" have not survived. The Philosophical Society did, however, authorise and fund the publication of "The Necessity for Political Honesty", delivered at the opening meeting of 1872. In the debating chamber of the

2

rival Historical Society, the author's career is, again, well-documented. It appears that, whatever his personal politics, he adopted a solidly conservative stance in debate, speaking against motions including, "That Vote by Ballot is Desirable", "That the Social and Political Disabilities of Women Ought to be Removed", and "That England Should Prepare for an early Emancipation of Her Colonies". Significantly, given his later contributions to the London journal *The Nineteenth Century,* he is also listed as a speaker against a motion, "That the Novels of the Nineteenth Century are More Immoral in their Tendency than those of the Eighteenth."[12] The College debating chamber thus appears to be the forum in which the author won his "medals, or certificates", gaining two silver medals from the Historical Society and a Certificate in Oratory from the Philosophical Society between 1869 and 1870.[13]

Stoker's career as a university athlete was equally distinguished. The author is listed as a member of the Dublin University Football Club Second Fifteen for the 1867-8 and 1868-9 seasons. In the lists for the 1869-70 and 1870-1 seasons he is noted as a member of the First Fifteen. Caps were awarded for distinguished play in College Rugby Football from 1867, although all games were played within the College — against the Rowing Club or the Law School, for example — until the 1871-2 season. Stoker, it appears, never became the Dublin equivalent of an Oxbridge "Blue".[14] The "numerous silver cups" mentioned by the author in *Personal Reminiscences of Henry Irving* were awarded for his victories in the Dublin University Foot Races and Seven Mile Walking Race of 1866 and 1868 respectively, and for his success at weightlifting in the Dublin University Gymnasium in 1870.[15]

Bram Stoker, it appears, was a popular, willing and able participant in the physical and overwhelmingly masculine culture of Trinity College in the eighteen-sixties and eighteen-seventies.[16] His experiences at Trinity, it may be argued, concretised the competitive and intellectual attitudes instilled into him during his youth. His graduation was thus another milestone in a process of acculturation which prepared the individual for acceptance within a society of gentlemen sharing similar aspirations and common standards of behaviour. These standards, their relevance to the relative positions of the sexes in Western society, and their apparent ability to transcend the boundaries of race and nationality, were to inform Stoker's writings from *A Glimpse of America* to *The Lair of the White Worm.*

The author's success in mobilising the discourses of the Anglo-Irish ascendancy would appear to be affirmed by his appointment to a Civil Service post within Dublin Castle in 1870, and again by his subsequent promotion to the office of Inspector of Petty Sessions in 1877. In this latter position, Stoker was to research and complete his first published work, *Duties of Clerks of Petty Sessions in Ireland,* a reference book for civil servants working within the Irish legal system. It is during this period, also, that the author's political beliefs appear to have crystallised, leading him by 1880 to a belief in the principles of Irish Home Rule, and eventually to membership of the National Liberal Club in London.[17] There is no evidence to suggest that Stoker ever viewed himself as part of a political or cultural consciousness beyond that possible within an integrated United Kingdom. This apparent lack of an explicit commitment to anything beyond a Liberal conception of Home Rule, coupled with a presumed literary alignment with what W.J. McCormack calls "the London exiles... as against the home-based revivalists", has ensured Stoker's exclusion from the heavily-politicised Irish canon of modern criticism.[18] The perception of the author upon which this exclusion is based, however, points again to the nature of Stoker's education and social training — both of which, it may be argued, minimised the disruption of his transition from Dublin society to that of London.

During the early years of his service within Dublin Castle Stoker began to draft a series of short stories, though with little immediate success. Though he published a fantasy, "The Crystal Cup", in a London-based periodical in 1872, a letter by the author dated 6 October 1874, reveals that another short story, "Jack Hammon's Vote", (now lost) was refused in turn by *The Cornhill Magazine*, *Macmillan's Magazine*, *Temple Bar* and *Blackwood's*.[19] The author was, however, to successfully place three serial pieces with *The Shamrock*, a Dublin weekly, in 1875. Stoker met with a more favourable reception as the anonymous (and, for the most part, unpaid) dramatic critic for the *Dublin Mail*, from 1871.[20] His experiences as a critic, with the social and political contacts made through his continuing membership of the Philosophical and Historical Societies, appear to have served as the qualifications which obtained for him the editorship of a short-lived evening periodical, *The Irish Echo*, first published on 6 November 1873.[21] He was to resign his editorship four months later, as the periodical, by then renamed *The Halfpenny Press*, ran into financial difficulties. Stoker was, though, to return to commercial periodical writing. He was an occasional contributor to the London *Daily Telegraph*, specialising in the public activities of well-known theatrical personalities, although his motives here appear to have been linked to publicity and to his social connection with the editor, rather than pecuniary gain.[22] He supplied articles on the theatre and literature to the London monthly *The Nineteenth Century* between 1890 and 1911 — again, it might appear, partly as a consequence of his friendship with the journal's editor, James Knowles. With the publisher William Heinemann he was a partner in the latter's venture into English-language publishing for the Continental Market, a rival to the Tauchnitz series marketed under the imprint of Heinemann and Balestier.[23] Finally, during his later years, when his finances were at a low ebb, he supplied a series of illustrated interviews, again with old associates, for a popular London newspaper, *The Daily Chronicle*.

Much of Stoker's non-fictional writing, as has been suggested, concerned the theatre. The central figure in Stoker's theatrical cosmology was the Victorian actor-manager, Henry (later, Sir Henry) Irving. Stoker's description of his first protracted encounter with the man who was to become his professional and social associate is frequently quoted but bears repeating. At an after-dinner gathering of a dozen men, Irving recited Thomas Hood's dramatic narrative poem *The Dream of Eugene Aram*, physically collapsing at its climax. Stoker confides:

As to its effect, I had no adequate words. I can only say that after a
few seconds of stony silence following his collapse I burst out into
something like a violent fit of hysterics.... In those moments of our
mutual emotion he too had found a friend and knew it. Soul had
looked into soul! From that hour began a friendship as profound, as
close, as lasting as can be between two men.[24]

It has been argued that Stoker's perception of his relationship with Irving differed
markedly from that perceived by the actor.[25] The author's insistence upon the
strongly homosocial bond which, he argued, persisted between himself and Irving is,
however, mirrored in at least two of the obituaries that followed Stoker's death. *The
New York Times* noted that:

As the *fidus Achates* of Henry Irving, and later as his Boswell, Bram
Stoker, who has just died in London, gained international fame....
Irving placed implicit confidence in Stoker's judgement and business
sense, while Stoker looked upon Irving as the only supremely great
man in the world.[26]

Elsewhere, the Manx novelist, Hall Caine, a close friend of both men, argued in
favour of the author's version of the relationship:

Much has been said of his relation to Henry Irving, but I wonder how
many were really aware of the whole depth and significance of that
association. Bram seemed to give up his life to it.... I say without any
hesitation that never have I seen, never do I expect to see, such
absorption of one man's life in the life of another.[27]

It would seem, therefore, that the public viewed Stoker largely as an appendage of
Irving, or of the Lyceum Theatre, rather than as an individual in his own right.[28] A
report of Stoker's attempt to rescue a Thames suicide, for example, describes the
author as Irving's "faithful Bram".[29] Stoker appears to have fostered this impression
so that, as Ellen Terry concedes, in the *Personal Reminiscences of Henry Irving*, the
author "described everyone connected with the Lyceum except himself."[30]

Irving invited Stoker to become his Acting Manager following a visit to
Dublin towards the close of 1878. Stoker's acceptance of Irving's offer caused him
to bring forward the date of his marriage to Florence Balcombe, who numbered Oscar
Wilde among her former suitors.[31] The author was to retain his position, which made
him Irving's accountant, secretary, and public spokesman for twenty-seven years, until
the actor's death in 1905. There is evidence to suggest that Stoker wrote at least some
of the speeches delivered by the actor between 1878 and 1905. A letter written by
L.F. Austin, Irving's private secretary, dated simply March 1885, reveals further that
Stoker was the author of an article published that year under Irving's name in *The
Fortnightly Review*.[32] Stoker was the major practical organiser of the Lyceum
Company's provincial seasons, and of eight tours made in the United States. Eight of
the author's novels, including *Dracula*, were therefore completed on a part-time basis
during Stoker's working lifetime. Irving's death, which came at the end of a long
period of physical debilitation and financial hardship, signalled the beginning of what
may be read as a consequent decline in Stoker's personal fortunes. Quite simply, the

author had made little professional or financial provision for a life outside of the theatre. Stoker's health, also, was by this time in visible decline. It has been stated that he was a sufferer from Bright's Disease (nephritis) as early as 1897.[33] At the beginning of 1906 the author also experienced a paralytic stroke which prostrated him for some months, and left him with disturbed vision. He appears to have experienced a further collapse, which he explains as the consequence of overwork, in 1909 or 1910.[34]

It was during the forced convalescence following his stroke that Stoker researched and wrote *Personal Reminiscences of Henry Irving*, the biography for which the author's contemporaries believed he would be chiefly remembered.[35] Though this work, which was republished within twelve months in a cheaper edition, was on the whole a commercial success, it could in no way be considered as the financial foundation of a second career in the wake of Irving's demise. The paperback volume of theatrical short stories, *Snowbound*, and the romantic novel, *Lady Athlyne*, both published in 1908, appear to have brought the author little financial reward, neither reaching a second edition. Stoker, therefore, embarked upon a succession of new ventures, each of which taxed his waning energy whilst bringing him limited remuneration. He became the business manager to a West End musical production of *The Vicar of Wakefield*, scripted by Laurence Housman and produced by the American opera singer, David Bispham. The production closed after two months. He then undertook a lecture tour in the English provinces which terminated, apparently at short notice, in Sheffield. Finally, he gained a short appointment as organiser of the British section of the 1908 Paris Theatrical Exhibition. At the same time, he was active in commercial journalism, publishing a number of non-fictional articles in the United Kingdom and the United States, and a series of interviews in the London press. This was, indeed, his most productive phase as a writer of fiction: just under half of his fictional publications came to fruition within a period of seven years. But the financial rewards were, again, light compared with the output.

By 1911 Stoker faced an acute financial crisis. As his application for a grant from the Royal Literary Fund reveals, his income was now significantly dependent upon his work as an author. Stoker's income for 1910, according to his application, totalled £409 from investments, and just over £166 from literary work, including, presumably, the advance for his final novel, *The Lair of the White Worm*.[36] The Committee of the Royal Literary Fund, after considering Stoker's application and the letters of reference supplied by Anne Ritchie, Henry F. Dickens and W. S. Gilbert, awarded the author a grant of £100 on 9 March 1911. He was, however, by this time terminally ill. He died at his home in Pimlico, London, on 20 April 1911, leaving his whole estate, which had a net value of just over £4,664, to his wife. Although one biographer has argued that the author was a victim of tertiary syphilis, the death certificate, with its enigmatic coda, "exhaustion", is far from conclusive.[37] Stoker was cremated following a quiet service at Golders Green, London, which was attended by Hall Caine, Genevieve Ward, Ford Madox Hueffer and Laurence Irving, the actor's second son.

Stoker's obituary in *The Times* conceded that, though the author would most likely be remembered for his biography of Irving, he was also "the master of a particularly lurid and creepy kind of fiction, represented by *Dracula* and other novels."[38] That said, it must be stated that only five of Stoker's eleven novels — *Dracula* (1897), *The Mystery of the Sea* (1902), *The Jewel of Seven Stars* (1903), *The Lady of the Shroud* (1909), and *The Lair of the White Worm* (1911) — may be regarded as unequivocally Gothic. In addition, two of the author's three volumes of short fiction — *Under the Sunset* (1882) and the posthumous *Dracula's Guest* (1914) — draw perceptibly (though not exclusively) upon Gothic and supernatural motifs. The remaining novels, together with much of the short and serial fiction, can be classified as popular romances which embody on occasion elements characteristic of the Gothic novel or of the late-Victorian adventure story. The whole range of Stoker's fiction is, however, informed by a fairly consistent complex of themes and discourses, most of which may be related without irony back to the author's cultural environment.

The author's construction of heroic masculinity, for example, is largely dependent on a conception of *mens sana in corpore sano* similar to that mentioned in connection with his own university career in *Personal Reminiscences of Henry Irving*.[39] It is a complex of signification which draws on a Spartan doctrine of self-improvement through struggle, similar to that expounded in Book Three of Carlyle's *Past and Present*:

> Here too thou shalt be strong of heart, noble of soul; thou shalt dread
> no pain or death, thou shalt not love ease or life.... thou shalt be a
> Knight and not a Chactaw, if thou wouldst prevail![40]

The key phrase here is "thou shalt not love ease". Stoker's heroes frequently undertake purgative and intensely physical journeys into the wilderness in order to attain or to recover their manhood. Rupert Sent Leger in *The Lady of the Shroud*, for example, travels to Madagascar and to the Himalayas, in order to effect a *rite de passage* from childhood dependency to adult independence. Rafe Otwell in *Miss Betty*, goes out, in his own words, "to purge my sin and to win honour again", and recovers his sense of chivalry whilst fighting against Turkish slavery in the East.[41] Harold AnWolf, the hero of *The Man*, discharges what he perceives as the baser qualities of his nature through toil in the Yukon. Arthur Severn in Stoker's first novel, *The Snake's Pass*, is able, similarly, to consider the coast of County Clare as a symbolic border country to be developed by hard work and colonialist ingenuity. All return from their experience morally and physically strengthened, transformed into fitting partners for the courageous women they will ultimately marry. Such activities are, therefore, crucial to the basic romantic script that characterises much of the author's fiction. As Harold is informed in *The Man*, by such struggles "You will prove yourself, your manhood, your worthiness to love and be loved".[42] The implication is that such periods of physical and mental endurance constitute the final gesture in a process of self-development: they are a modern version of the knightly vigil.

On attaining their manhood, Stoker's heroes become at times self-conscious participants in the Victorian and Edwardian discourse of modern chivalry. The principle of chivalric activity penetrates the concept of the hero, making him also a gentleman, his actions as well as his morals a reflection, not always explicit, of a knightly ideal. The emblematically-named English hero Arthur Severn, for example, amuses himself by quoting Tennyson's courtly Idyll, *Enid*, and engages finally in the chivalric defence of an Irish maiden beset by a rapacious and greedy neighbour, one of her own countrymen. Arthur Holmwood, Lord Godalming, in *Dracula*, similarly shares a concern for what he describes as "my honour as a gentleman [and] my faith as a Christian" and, indeed, mobilises both during his membership of a group of essentially errant males, banded together in defence of a vulnerable female "as the old Knights of the Cross", in Van Helsing's words.[43] Similar motivations characterise the majority of Stoker's heroes, who are, for the best part, professional or titled men — barristers, doctors, landowners, or professional soldiers. Chivalric behaviour — or "natural" chivalry — is not exclusively determined by social class, however. "Sailor" Willy Barrow, in the Scottish tale *The Watter's Mou'*, is tempted by a romantic involvement to neglect his duties as a coastguard. His rejection of the temptation, and devotion both to his professional honour and to the heroine, with whom he is subsequently found drowned, is again characteristic of an approved pattern of male behaviour in the author's fiction. Chivalry, it appears, is a common standard of behaviour which, when recognised or displayed, may excite the empathy of similar men across all social classes.

Chivalry and masculinity function equally, however, as motifs through which racial issues may be channelled, in such a way as to provide a point of intersection between the portrayed aspirations of the British and other culturally "Western" nations. On one level, Stoker's fictionalisation of the racial questions of his day draws upon the motif of struggle in self-development, and considers its possible relationship to the renewal or expansion of the nation. The purified hero, when recognised as such, may become a leader of men:

> ... the men around closed in upon the Gospodar like a wave of the sea, and in a second held him above their heads, tossing on their lifted hands as if on stormy breakers. It was as though the old vikings of whom we have heard, and whose blood flows in Rupert's veins, were choosing a chief in old fashion.

Hence, Rupert Sent Leger's activities in the Balkans lead to the restructuring of a non-aligned country into "an ally of Britain — who will stand at least as an outpost of our nation".[44] The alliance is based on a recognition not merely of strong leadership, but on a common racial heritage and identity also. A recurrent pattern of colonization effected essentially in reverse, however, occurs elsewhere in Stoker's fiction: male members of the Anglo-Saxon race reared abroad return to the "home country", where their presence (and ultimately marriage within the local community) renews the local racial stock. Adam Salton, the Australian-born hero of *The Lair of the White Worm*, for example, returns to England as heir of the last-remaining member of his family — or, as his uncle terms it, of "our race".[45] Once in England, his colonial

8

resourcefulness becomes a crucial factor in the downfall of a degenerate aristocrat whose occult activities threaten the region. The Texan, Quincey Morris, fulfils a broadly similar rôle in *Dracula*. A major implication embedded in writings of this type is that the Anglo-Saxon raised overseas in a pioneering spirit embodies in his character a vision of personal and national culture that is in decline at the centre of the Empire. The essence of racial identity and achievement is thus brought home to act as a catalyst on a nation moving slowly towards decline. Chivalry is again a crucial factor in this cultural renaissance, particularly in the author's construction of characters born in the United States. Stoker states in his early monograph, *A Glimpse of America*, for example, that:

> One of the most marked characteristics of American Life is the high regard in which woman is held. It seems, now and then, as if a page of an old book of chivalry had been taken as the text of a social law.[46]

Modern chivalry, in a sense, has overwritten race and in so doing has affirmed the racial tie. The maturity and lineage of the United States as "England's first-born child" (to recall a phrase from *A Glimpse of America*) is thus verified through the unfeigned and spontaneous masculine chivalry of what Stoker sees as its representative classes.[47] Beyond the fictionalisation of American manhood, it is notable also that the author elsewhere scripts three of his British heroes — Archibald Hunter in *The Mystery of the Sea*, Lord Athlyne in *Lady Athlyne*, and Reginald Hampden in *The Shoulder of Shasta* — as marrying American heroines. Again, the racial and political implications are clear; as indeed they are in the marriage between the emblematically named Balkan heroine, Teuta, and the British adventurer, Rupert Sent Leger, in *The Lady of the Shroud*.

Stoker's fictionalisation of the female and of female sexuality is, to a certain extent, dependent upon the same racial discourses that structure his heroes. Though his heroines at first sight embody the prevalent nineteenth-century view of a destiny and temperament determined in the first instance by personal biology, it is apparent that gender in Stoker's novels exists in an often tense relationship with race. When under threat, Teuta, in *The Lady of the Shroud*, takes up arms with a teutonic militancy that echoes her Christian name. In less warlike circumstances, however, she is, in her own words, "as any other wife in our land, equal to them in domestic happiness, which is our woman's sphere... an exemplar of woman's rectitude."[48] As an inheritor of "the blood of forty generations of loyal women", her submission to the male is thus not a denial of "the fighting blood of her race" but, perversely, its ironic affirmation.[49] Similar behaviour is exhibited by the American heroines of *Lady Athlyne* and *The Mystery of the* Sea, both of whom, following a period of personal initiative, submit without resistance to the directives of their marital partners. Arguably, race is a resource which may be drawn upon in times of crisis. Gender, which, Stoker argues, inspires in the Anglo-Saxon woman both modesty and submission, is, however, both unavoidable and the most powerful factor in the individual's character, reasserting its dominance as soon as the crisis is over.

The crises which are endured by Stoker's heroines exist, however, essentially as opportunities for the physical and emotional display of the female. In consequence, the sexual threats to which the heroines are subjected trace a fine line between prurience and outrage. There are implications of possible rape written into the abductions in *The Lady of the Shroud* and *The Mystery of the Sea*, and an oblique though protracted scene of seduction in *Lady Athlyne*. Again, in a similarly protracted scene in *The Jewel of Seven Stars*, the hero witnesses the display of the naked body of Tera, an Egyptian Queen who is the physiological double of his fiancée. The outraged modesty of the fiancée, notably, brings the scene to a close as she forcibly covers the prone body. Elsewhere, Mina Harker's sexualised submission to the vampire Count, the apparent sexual rapacity of the dying Lucy Westenra in *Dracula*, and the marriage proposal issued as a polemical gesture by Stephen Norman in *The Man*, provide an ironic suggestion of apparently uncharacteristic though short-lived erotic urges in heroines who are rapidly restored to a conventional passivity by the exercise of masculine power. Stoker's texts function in such cases rather in the manner of a rhetorical question. The heroines are displayed at the brink of real or encoded sexual transgression, or in the act of self-abasement. The narratives subsequently restore them to penitence or to a retraction of their waywardness, and finally to a culturally conventional modesty — through marriage, or, in the case of Lucy, through another coded sexual act. Perversely, Stoker's heroines are both erotic and virginal, morally innocent and yet sexually aware: it is the final closure of each text, therefore, that ensures their continued cultural acceptance as, to recall Van Helsing's words, "sweet, sweet, good, good" women.[50]

It is easy to categorise Stoker as a hack writer, and easier to suggest that his writings before and after *Dracula* are unexceptionable, participating in rather than challenging the dominant discourses of his day.[51] This is a consequence of the emphasis placed by the critical establishment upon a single text. But, it may be argued, the author's manipulation of his materials is frequently effected in such a way as to produce not merely irony in the midst of supposed conventionality, but at times a marked redirection of their discursive energy. One example must suffice here. In *Dracula* the author constructs a psychology for the vampire which, as Mina Harker recognises, may have been drawn without comment from the writings of Cesare Lombroso and Max Nordau. Daniel Pick, Ernest Fontana and Victor Sage have argued that the physiognomy of Dracula is intimate to this portrayed psychology.[52] Stoker's vampire is, in nineteenth-century cultural terms, a multiplex signifier of personal and racial degeneration: the pointed ears and squat fingers suggest the ape, the "peculiarly sharp white teeth" and pointed fingernails signify predatory, carnivorous appetites, the pallor and hairy palms recall the "degenerate" behaviour of the modern-day onanist.[53] But at the same time, the vampire signifies in his person qualities that, though loathsome, are perversely admirable. Harker's admiration is thinly veiled, for example, in his admission that the Count displayed "astonishing vitality in a man of his years"; Van Helsing's is even less so in his assessment of Dracula's achievement:

He have done this alone; all alone! from a ruin tomb in a forgotten land. What more may he not do when the greater world of thought is open to him?[54]

More than one set of evaluative criteria is clearly in use here. The vampire is "degenerate", and yet is poised to equal, if not surpass, those who have judged him so. Arguably, the fascination and admiration of both commentators comes from an appreciation of his abstract *power*, so that the signifiers of degeneration, being at the same time signifiers of difference, have their cultural or discursive energy redirected.

Count Dracula, however, is but one of several similarly-constructed characters in Stoker's fiction. Indeed, Don Bernardino de Escoban in *The Mystery of the Sea* is, arguably, a more complex figure in that he is both mortal and a participant in contemporary politics. Like Count Dracula, the Don is a nobleman of ancient family, and displays an explicitly "cruel" aquiline countenance:

As he spoke, the canine teeth began to show. He knew what he had to tell was wrong; and being determined to brazen it out, the cruelty which lay behind his strength became manifest at once. Somehow at that moment the racial instinct manifested itself.[55]

Unlike Dracula, however, the Don is a participant in the same discourse of chivalric masculinity that mobilises the novel's hero, Archibald Hunter. Don Bernardino's physiognomy, like that of the vampire, is awesome in that it is the visible manifestation of the qualities that permit the survival of a dynasty, that allow an individual to cross the centuries in reputation, if not in the characteristics inherited by his descendants.[56] The racial inheritance, which is closely aligned here with familial identity, becomes a resource upon which both men may draw in the interests of survival.

This resource, however, must remain a reserve, rather than becoming a predominant principle for personal action. In *Personal Reminiscences of Henry Irving*, the author renders Alfred, Lord Tennyson, through a similar process of signification:

Tennyson had at times that lifting of the upper lip which shows the canine tooth, and which is so marked an indication of militant instinct.[57]

The association of these elsewhere cruel, atavistic or degenerate qualities with a specific standard of manliness is thus the determining factor both in the description of Tennyson, and in that of the fictional Don Bernardino. The self-restraint, altruism and respect for the female associated with the conventional encoding of the gentleman ensures that these "degenerate" qualities are restrained until needed. Given purpose by circumstances, they become a potential upon which the gentleman may draw in the name or cause of honour, above and beyond the demands of personal survival. With his commitment to chivalry ratified by his death in defence of the heroine, the Don loses in the final account his cultural negativity. As is frequently the case with Stoker's heroines, a conflict between race and gender has seemingly been enacted. The fighting attributes of the race, signified by the exposure of the explicitly "cruel" canine tooth, are held in check by a chivalry that is, by its spontaneity, both "natural" and hereditary. The cultural energy of the signifier has thus, apparently, been turned back upon itself.

This introduction has, to a great extent, set itself self-consciously against the two major characteristics of modern Stoker criticism: namely, the frequently aired conclusions that the author was a hack writer, and that *Dracula* was his only achievement. It has sought to avoid, also, the psychobiographical approach that has characterised much of the published criticism examining Stoker's texts, and has attempted to return the texts to the Victorian and Edwardian cultural context in which the author was a participant. With the approach of the centenary of *Dracula* in 1997, there has never been a better opportunity to reappraise not merely Stoker, but also the technique of criticism currently employed in a limited though undeniably fruitful area of the critical field.

III

This Bibliography aims to list each distinguishable edition of Stoker's books, noting the occurrence of variations in title, subtitle, or the style of the author's name. It cannot, however, pretend to provide a comprehensive handlist of the author's publications, particularly in the case of *Dracula*. In many cases minimal — if any — changes separate publications designated as "new" or different editions by their publishers. For example, in 1895 *The Shoulder of Shasta* was issued in Macmillan's Colonial Library using the printing plates created for the Constable First Edition.[58] The various reprints published over a period of almost fifteen years by Jarrolds and Arrow similarly betray through their pagination a limited range of changes. Each edition listed within the bibliography, however, shows some variation on the title page or verso — if only the announcement of a new edition or the incorporation of a revised publication date. Pagination details for the volumes listed have been included wherever possible, although it is regretted that information regarding some of the more scarce material has been gained from sight of reproduced title pages supplied by libraries and archives, rather than from first-hand contact with the actual volumes. Reproductions of the title pages of all of Stoker's British First Editions may be found in Richard Dalby's excellent study, *Bram Stoker. A Bibliography of First Editions.*

Stoker's short stories, and his largely uncollected corpus of interviews and journalism have been listed in order of first publication. Two short stories uncovered since the publication of Dalby's *Bibliography of First Editions* are listed here for the first time, as is a previously unknown Introduction to a volume of fiction by Stoker's close friend Hall Caine. One or two pieces of short fiction — most notably the short story "In the Valley of the Shadow", first published in *The Grand Magazine* — have been listed only in their reprinted form, again because of the unavailability of the original periodicals. The same is true of the author's largely anonymous contributions to the Irish Press.

Stoker's personal library, manuscripts and paintings were disposed of by his widow through a series of three sales organised by Sotheby's of London. Of six manuscript items sold in the first sale of 1913, only one — the manuscript notes of *Dracula*, now in the Rosenbach Library and Museum, Philadelphia — remain in the public domain. The remainder, namely the manuscripts of *Personal Reminiscences of Henry Irving*, *The Lady of the Shroud*, *Under the Sunset*, *The Lair of the White Worm* and the last four stories in *Snowbound*, are presumably in private collections. Other items, including the bound manuscripts of "The Secret of the Growing Gold" and *A Glimpse of America*, and the first draft of *Miss Betty*, were sold at a second sale in 1915 to the London rare book dealers Maggs Brothers. Much of this material was eventually transferred to the Brotherton Collection, held at Leeds University Library. The incomplete manuscript of *Famous Imposters*, sold at the same sale, is now in the Library of Trinity College Dublin. Materials sold at the 1916 sale but never traced include the manuscript of an unpublished article on Tennyson, and the outline notes to *The Snake's Pass*. There are probably hundreds of manuscript letters by the author, mostly on theatrical matters, in private collections worldwide. Details of letters written to Stoker have been included in the Bibliography where these remain in the public domain.

The Bibliography has sought to include a wide range of contemporary review and obituary material. Passing references to Stoker in his capacity as Irving's Acting Manager can also be found in contemporary and modern studies of *fin-de-siècle* theatre culture, and in the theatre journals of the author's lifetime. This contemporary material has been supplemented by a detailed list of modern studies considering the author and his works. It must be remembered, however, that *Dracula* in particular is treated at shorter length in many studies of nineteenth-century fiction and culture.[59] The modern critical studies listed in this Bibliography are, inevitably, being supplemented continuously in response to the popular as well as scholarly interest in the author. With this in mind, I should be grateful for corrections and addenda from the files of other scholars active in the field.

*

Many friends and colleagues have drawn my attention to Stoker items, or to relevant material subsequently incorporated in this Bibliography. I should like to acknowledge in particular the assistance of Dr Antonio Ballasteros Gonzalez, Mr David Lass, Mr William Murphy, Ms Diane Mason, Dr Richard Deswarte, Mr Dennis McIntyre, Dr Graham Ford and Dr Robert Mighall, all of whom supplied information not available to me in Bath. I am also grateful for the support received from my colleagues at Bath College of Higher Education, and to Dr Neil Sammells, Dean of Humanities, for making research funds available for this project. Special thanks go also to Dr Jeff Rodman, to Ms Sarah Briggs, and to Mr Ian Lovell of the BCHE Computing Centre. I am grateful also for the advice and support supplied by Ms Alita Thorpe, Dr Victor Sage, Dr Roger Sales, Dr Mary C. Lyons, Dr Andy Smith and Martin and Anna Wrigley.

This Bibliography could not have been completed without the assistance of th many libraries, whose staff have made available, frequently at short notice, rar manuscript material and obscure reprints. These include the Libraries of the Universit of East Anglia, Trinity College Dublin, Cambridge University, Ohio State Universit and the University of Mississippi, as well as the Bodleian Library, the Nationa Library of Ireland, the Brotherton Collection at Leeds University, the Rosenbac Library, Philadelphia and the Deutsche Bibliothek, Frankfurt.

Finally, I would like to dedicate this Bibliography to two people whose suppo has been both consistent and honest: Elaine Hartnell and Benjamin Fisher.

William Hughes
Bath, December 199€

Notes

1. Alain Garsault, "Review of *Bram Stoker. Prince des Ténèbres*", *Positif* 353 (19 128.

2. E.g. Daniel Farson, *The Man Who Wrote Dracula*, London: Michael Joseph, I pp.233-5.

3. For example, *Dracula A.D. 1972*, (U.K.: Hammer, 1972). See: Leslie Shepard, "E Stoker and the Cinema", *The Bram Stoker Society Journal* 7 (1995): 2-12.

4. Bela Lugosi played the title role in the 1931 Universal Pictures production of *Dracula*, the first film of the novel produced with the permission of Stoker's widow.

5. Bram Stoker, *Personal Reminiscences of Henry Irving*, 2 Vols., London: Wil Heinemann, 1906, Vol.1, p.31.

6. Entry number 62 in the Parish Register of the church of St. John the Baptist, Clontarf, Dublin.

7. For an account of the culture of formal education in this period see: M. Girouar *The Return to Camelot. Chivalry and the English Gentleman*, London: Yale University Press, 1981, pp.164-76; J.R. de S. Honey, *Tom Brown's Universe. Th Development of the Public School in the Nineteenth Century*, London: Millingto 1977, passim.

8. Under the regulations of the University of Dublin, candidates deemed to have passed their degree with Honours were termed "Moderators". Candidates for ordinary degrees who had passed with special merit were awarded "Respondenc

A search of the Muniment Records of the University of Dublin, dated between 1864 and 1880, reveals that Stoker was not awarded either distinction.

9.   Stoker 1906, Vol.1, p.32.

10. E.g., D.R. Perry, "Whitman's Influence on Stoker's *Dracula*", *Walt Whitman Quarterly Review* 3 (1986): 29-35.

11. Undergraduate Philosophical Society, Trinity College, Dublin, *Minute Book 1861-7*. Entry dated 7 May 1868.

12. *College Historical Society Address*, 1872, Appendix, p.51 [National Library of Ireland: P.1399(20)].

13. See: *College Historical Society Address*, 1872, Appendix, pp.40-1; *Undergraduate Philosophical Society Minute Book* 1861-7, 25 Nov 1869.

14. The Committee of the Dublin University Football Club, *Dublin University Football Club 1854-1954*, Dublin: Mountford, 1954, pp.50-2, p.65.

15. Farson 1975, p.18. Farson also notes a further cup presented in 1868 by the CSAS — possibly the Athletics society of the Irish Civil Service.

16. See: C. Sweeting, "Bram Stoker", in J.P. Cinnamond ed., *University Philosophical Society, Trinity College Dublin, Centenary Review*, Dublin: The Centenary Committee of the Philosophical Society, 1953, p.52.

17. Stoker 1906, Vol.1, p.343; *Who Was Who*, London: A & C Black, 1935, p.680.

18. W.J. McCormack, "Irish Gothic and After (1820-1945)", in S. Deane ed., *The Field Day Anthology of Irish Writing*, Vol. 2, Londonderry: Field Day, 1991, p.845.

19. National Library of Scotland: MS4325 *f.*240.

20. Stoker 1906, Vol. 1, p.13. Stoker's early theatre criticism is almost impossible to trace with accuracy due to the modern-day scarcity of the periodicals to which he was a contributor. A few extracts are, however, reprinted in *Personal Reminiscences of Henry Irving*. The volume also includes his *Dublin Mail* account of the University Night held in honour of Irving at the Theatre Royal Dublin on 11 Dec 1876: Stoker 1906, Vol. 1, p.22, pp.26-7, pp.37-40.

21. H. Ludlam, *A Biography of Dracula. The Life Story of Bram Stoker*, London: Foulsham, 1962, pp.33-4.

22. Stoker 1906, Vol. 1, p.287.

23. See: John St. John, *William Heinemann, A Century of Publishing 1890-1990*, Lond Heinemann, 1990, p.20.

24. The incident took place on the evening of 3 Dec 1876: Stoker 1906, Vol. 1, pp.3

25. L. Irving, *Henry Irving. The Actor and His World*, London: Columbus Books, 19 p.453, cf. p.444; E. Terry, "First Years at the Lyceum. The Story of What He Irving did for the English Stage", *McClure's Magazine* 30 (1908): 374.

26. *The New York Times*, 23 April 1912: 12.

27. Hall Caine, "Bram Stoker. The Story of a Great Friendship", *The Daily Telegraph*, April 1912: 16. Caine, as "Hommy Beg", was the dedicatee of *Dracula*, as he expla in this obituary account of Stoker's life.

28. Witness the title of Stoker's obituary in *The Daily Telegraph*, "Death of Mr. Bra Stoker. Sir H. Irving's Manager", *The Daily Telegraph*, 22 April 1912: 6.

29. *The Entr'acte*, 23 Sept 1882: 4, cf. Caine 1912, p.16.

30. Terry 1908, p.374.

31. The Stokers were married at St. Ann's Church, Dublin, on 4 Dec 1878 [Entry number 120 in the Church Register]. For correspondence connected with the relationship between Oscar Wilde and Florence Balcombe see: Farson 1975, pp.4 2, pp.60-1.

32. Item 316 in this Bibliography. See: Irving 1989, pp.452-3.

33. Farson 1975, p.232.

34. See: Stoker's letter to the Committee of the Royal Literary Fund, dated 25 Feb 1911, held at the British Library, London: British Library M1077/117 [Correspondence of the Royal Literary Fund, File 2841].

35. See: "Bram Stoker", *The New York Times*, 23 April 1912: 12.; Caine 1912, p.16.

36. British Library M1077/117.

37. Farson 1975, pp.233-5, cf. p.223.

38. "Death of Mr. Bram Stoker", *The Times* 22 April 1912: 15, rpt in Ludlam 1962, p.150.

39. Stoker 1906, Vol. 1, p.32.

40. Thomas Carlyle, *Past and Present*, ed. A.M.D. Hughes, Oxford: Clarendon, 192 p.172.

41. Bram Stoker, *Miss Betty*, London: C. Arthur Pearson, 1898, p.176

42. Bram Stoker, *The Man*, London: William Heinemann, 1905, p.318.

43. Bram Stoker, *Dracula*, Oxford: Oxford University Press, 1983, p.205, cf. p.314; p.320

44. Bram Stoker, *The Lady of the Shroud*, London: William Heinemann, 1909, p.230, p.297

45. Bram Stoker, *The Lair of the White Worm*, rpt in *Dracula* and *The Lair of the White Worm*, London: Foulsham, 1986, p.336.

46. Bram Stoker, *A Glimpse of America*, London: Sampson Low, Marston, 1886, p.28.

47. Stoker 1886, p.47.

48. Stoker 1909, pp.319-20, cf. pp.227-8.

49. Stoker 1909, p.319, p.240.

50. Stoker 1983, p.308.

51. See: A.N. Wilson's, "Introduction" to the Oxford University Press "World's Classics" series *Dracula*, Stoker 1983, p.x, p.xviii; cf. C. Leatherdale, *Dracula. The Novel and the Legend*, Northampton: Aquarian, 1985, pp.94-5.

52. Stoker 1983, p.342; D. Pick, "Terrors of the Night: *Dracula* and 'Degeneration' in the Late-Nineteenth Century", *Critical Quarterly* 30 (1988): 71-87; E. Fontana, "Lombroso's Criminal Man and Stoker's *Dracula*", *Victorian Newsletter* 66 (1984): 25-7; V. Sage, *Horror Fiction in the Protestant Tradition*, Basingstoke: Macmillan, 1988, pp.180-5.

53. Stoker 1983, pp.17-8.

54. Stoker 1983, p.17, p.321.

55. Bram Stoker, *The Mystery of the Sea*, London: William Rider, 1913, p.328.

56. Don Bernardino is portrayed throughout as the descendant of an earlier de Escoban, whose image is viewed supernaturally by Hunter. See also Stoker 1983, p.28-9, p.240.

57. Stoker 1906, Vol. 1, p.167.

58. R. Dalby, *Bram Stoker. A Bibliography of First Editions*, London: Dracula, 1983, p.22.

59. E.g., D. Punter, *The Literature of Terror* Vol.2, London: Longman, 1996, pp.15-22; S.M. Gilbert and S. Gubar, *No Man's Land*, Vol. 2, "Sexchanges", New Haven: Yale

University Press, 1989, pp.22-5; F. Botting, *Gothic*, London: Routledge, 1996, pp.145-54.

Primary Bibliography

Fiction

i. Novels and Collections of Shorter Fiction

The Snake's Pass

1. **The Snake's Pass** By Bram Stoker M.A.. London: Sampson Low, Marston, Searle and Rivington, 1891 [Published 18 Nov 1890]. 356p.

2. New York: Harper (Franklin Square Library New Series, number 685), 1890. 234p.

3. London: Sampson Low, 1892.

4. "New and Cheaper Edition". London: Collier (Collier's Shilling Library), 1909. 365p.

5. Dingle: Brandon, 1990. 256p.

6. "The Gombeen Man" [i.e. "Chapter 3"], rpt in Charles Osborne ed., *The Bram Stoker Bedside Companion*, London: Victor Gollancz, 1973, pp.151-65.

7. "The Gombeen Man" [i.e. "Chapter 3"], rpt in Peter Haining ed., *Midnight Tales*, London: Peter Owen, 1990, pp.71-84.

The Man from Shorrox'

8. **"The Man from Shorrox'"**, *The Pall Mall Magazine* 2 (Feb 1894): 656-69.

9. New York: Theo. L. DeVinne, 1894. 21p.

10. "The Man from Shorrox'", rpt in Peter Haining ed., *Midnight Tales*, London: Peter Owen, 1990, pp.107-19.

Crooken Sands

11. **Crooken Sands** by Bram Stoker. New York: Theo L. DeVinne, 1894. 31p.

12. "Crooken Sands", *The Illustrated Sporting and Dramatic News* Christmas Issue ("Holly Leaves"), 1 Dec 1894: 28-32

The Watter's Mou'

13. **The Watter's Mou'** by Bram Stoker. New York: Theo L. DeVinne, 1894. 82p.

14. Westminster: A. Constable (The Acme Library), 1895. 165p.

15. New York: Appleton, 1895. 178p.

16. Rpt in Charles Osborne ed., *The Bram Stoker Bedside Companion*, London: Victor Gollancz, 1973, pp.166-224.

The Shoulder of Shasta

17. **The Shoulder of Shasta** by Bram Stoker. Westminster: Archibald Constable, 1895. 235p.

18. London and New York: Macmillan (Macmillan's Colonial Library, number 230), 1895. 235p.

Dracula

19. **Dracula** by Bram Stoker. Westminster: Archibald Constable, 1897. 390p.

20. New York: Doubleday and McClure, 1899. 378p.

21. London: Archibald Constable, 1901. [Paperback edition]

22. New York: A. Wessells, 1901.

23. *Makt Myrkranna* "eftir Bram Stoker. Þytt hefir [i.e. trans] Valdimar Ásmundsson". Reykjavik: Nokkrir Prentarar, 1901. 220p. [Abridged edition]

24. New York: Doubleday, Page, 1909. 378p.

25. *Dracula. A Mystery Story.* New York: W.R. Caldwell (The International Adventure Library, Three Owls Edition), n.d. [c.1910-9]. 378p.

26. "Ninth Edition". London: William Rider, 1912. 404p.

27. "Tenth Edition". London: William Rider, 1913. 404p.

28. Garden City, New York: Doubleday, Page, 1913. 378p.

29. Garden City, New York: Doubleday, Page, 1919. 378p.

30. "Thirteenth Edition". London: William Rider, 1919. 404p.

31. Garden City, New York: Doubleday, Page, 1920. 378p.

32. Garden City, New York: Doubleday, Page (The Lambskin Library, number 6), 1925. 378p. [rpt 1927]

33. Garden City, New York: Doubleday, Page, 1927. 353p.

34. London: William Rider, 1927. 404p.

35. Garden City, New York: Garden City Publishing (The Sun Dial Library), n.d. [1928]. 354p.

36. New York: Grossett and Dunlap, 1928. 354p.

37. Garden City, New York: Doubleday, Page, 1929. 378p.

38. "With illustrations from the Universal Picture produced by Carl Laemmle, jr.". New York: Grossett and Dunlap, 1930. 354p.

39. *The Horror Omnibus, containing two complete novels* [*Dracula* and *Frankenstein*]. New York: Grossett and Dunlap, n.d.. pp.1-354.

40. Графъ Дракула. Sofia: Zarnitsky Publishing House, n.d. [c.1930]. 177p. [Russian language edition]

41. "First Modern Library Edition". New York: Modern Library (The Modern Library of the World's Best Books), 1932. 418p.

42. "Bram Stoker do scríobh, Seàn Ó Cuirrín do chuir [i.e. trans.] i nGaedhilg". Baile Átha Cliath: Oifig Díolta Foillseacháin Rialtais, 1933. 450p. [Irish language edition]

43. "Traduit de l'anglais par Eve et Lucie Paul Marguerite". Paris: Les Editions des Quatre-vents (Les maîtres du fantastique), 1946. 343p. [French language edition]

44. London: Arrow, 1954. 336p.

45. Garden City, New York: Garden City, 1959. 354p.

46. *Dracula. il vampiro*, Milano: Longanesi, 1959. [Italian language edition]

47. New York: Modern Library, n.d. [c.1960]. 418p.

48. *Drácula*, Barcelona: Ed. Saturno, 1962. [Spanish language edition]

49. "With an Introduction by Anthony Boucher, illustrated with wood engravings by Felix Hoffman". New York: Heritage, 1965. 410p.

50. "With an Introduction by Anthony Boucher, illustrated with wood engravings by Felix Hoffman". New York: The Limited Editions Club, 1965. 410p. [A numbered issue of 1,500 copies signed by the Illustrator at rear]

51. New York: Dell Publishing (The Laurel Leaf Library), 1965. 416p.

52. London: Arrow, 1965. 336p.

53. London: Jarrolds, 1966. 336p.

54. London: Hutchinson, 1966. 336p.

55. *Dracula. il vampiro*, "Traduzione di Adriana Pellegrini". Milano: Longanesi (i libri pocket, number 25), 1966. 323p. [Italian language edition]

56. *Drácula*. Barcelona: Ed. Molino, 1966. [Spanish language edition]

57. *Dracula. Ein Vampirroman*, "Vollstande Übersetzung des Textes der Ausg. von 1897 von Stasi Kull, unter Benutzung alterer Überträgungen". München: Hanser, 1967. 522p. [German language edition]

58. "Traduction de Lucienne Molitor. Pref. et Bibliographie de Gilbert Sigaux. Illus. originales et frontispièce de Christian Brouin". Levallois-Perret: Distribué par le Cercle du Bibliophile, 1968. 523p. [French language edition]

59. *Dracula. Ein Vampirroman*, "Vollstande Übersetzung des Textes nach der Ausg. von 1897 von Stasi Kull, unter Benutzung alterer Überträgungen". München: Deutscher Taschenbuch Verlag, 1968. 429p. [German language edition]

60. *Dracula. Roman.* Olten: Fackelverlag, 1968. 404p. [German language edition]

61. Trans. Fernando Trías, with a prologue by Pere Gimferrer. Barcelona: Táber, 1969. [Spanish language edition]

62. "With illustrations of the author and the setting of the story, together with an introduction by James Nelson". New York: Dodd, Mead (Great Illustrated Classics), 1970. 430p.

63. London: Hutchinson, 1970. 336p.

64. London: Arrow, 1970. 384p.

65. London: Hutchinson, 1972. 336p.

66. London: Arrow, 1974. 336p.

67. London: Sphere (The Dennis Wheatley Library of the Occult, number 1), 1974. 382p.

68. London: Hutchinson, 1975. 336p.

69. *The Annotated Dracula*, edited by Leonard Wolf, with illustrations by Sätty. New York: Clarkson N. Potter, 1975. 362p.

70. *The Annotated Dracula*, edited by Leonard Wolf. London: New English Library, 1975.

71. *The Illustrated Dracula.* New York: Drake, 1975. 184p.

72. *Dracula di Bram Stoker*, "Annotato da Leonard Wolf, Illustrato da Sätty. Traduzione di Adriana Pellegrini e Jimmy Boraschi". Milano: Longanesi, 1976. [Italian language edition]

73. *The Annotated Dracula*, edited by Leonard Wolf. New York: Ballantine, 1976. 362p.

74. Cutchogue, New York: Buccaneer, 1976. 382p.

75. "With illustrations from the 1979 Universal Picture". New York: Jove, 1979. 352p.

76. Harmondsworth: Penguin, 1979. 449p.

77. London: Arrow, 1979. 336p.

78. New York: Ace (A Tempo Star Book), 1979. 508p.

79. *The Essential Dracula, A Completely Illustrated and Annotated Edition of Bram Stoker's Classic Novel* by Raymond McNally and Radu Florescu. New York: Mayflower, 1979. 320p.

80. New York: Harcourt Brace Jovanovich (Jove Publications), 1979. 352p.

81. Paris: Le masque, 1979. [French language edition]

82. "Introduzione e traduzione di Francesco Saba Sardi". Milano: A. Mondadori Editore, 1979. 435p. [Italian language edition]

83. *Drácula*. Barcelona: Producciones Editoriales, D.L., 1979. 391p. [Spanish language edition]

84. *Dracula, by Bram Stoker* [and] *Frankenstein, or, The Modern Prometheus, by Mary Shelley*. Garden City, New York: International Collector's Library, n.d. [1980?]. 655p.

85. *Drácula*, translated by Mario Montalban. Esplugues de Llobregat (Barcelona): Plaza y Janés, 1980. 457p. [Spanish language edition, rpt 1986, 1990, 1992 (twice)]

86. "With an Introduction by George Stade". Toronto: Bantam, 1981. 402p.

87. *Dracula. Ein Vampirroman*. München: Deutscher Taschenbuch Verlag, 1981. 430p. [German language edition]

88. *Drácula*, translated by Francisco Torres Oliver. Barcelona: Bruguera (Libro amigo), 1981. 511p. [Spanish language edition]

89. "With an Introduction and Notes by A.N. Wilson". Oxford: Oxford University Press (The World's Classics), 1983. 380p.

90. "Roman Aus d. Engl.". München: Heyne [Heyne Taschenbuch number 524], 1984. 299p. [German language edition]

91. *Drácula*, translated by Fernando Trías. Two vols. Madrid: Fascículos Planeta (Aula), 1984. [Spanish language edition]

92. *Drácula*, translated by Flora Cass. Madrid: Edicones Generales Anaya, 1984. 398p. [Spanish language edition]

93. *Drácula*, translated by Fernando Trías. Barcelona: Planeta, 1984. [Spanish language edition]

94. *Drácula*, translated by Sílvia Aymerich. Barcelona: Laertes, 1984. 465p. [Catalan language edition, rpt 1989]

95. Edited by Fernado Fermandez. Paris: Campus, 1985. 94p. [Abridged French language edition]

96. Illustrated by Greg Hildebrandt. Parsippany, N.J.: Unicorn, n.d. [1985]. 261p.

97. *Drácula*, translated by Francisco Torres Oliver. Barcelona: Bruguera (Libro amigo), 1985. 490p. [Spanish language edition, rpt 1992]

98. *A Bram Stoker Omnibus Edition. Dracula and The Lair of the White Worm, Complete and Unabridged with New Original Material.* Introduction by Richard Dalby. London: W. Foulsham, 1986, pp.10-331.

99. Paris: Longman, 1987. 72p. [Abridged French language edition]

100. Paris: Marabout, 1987. 512p. [French language edition]

101. Illustrated by Charles Keeping. London: Blackie, 1988. 379p.

102. New York: Bedrick, 1989. 368p.

103. *Classics of Horror* [*Dracula* and *Frankenstein*]. Stamford CT: Longmeadow, 1991. 654p.

104. *Bram Stoker's Dracula Omnibus. Dracula, The Lair of the White Worm, Dracula's Guest.* Introduction by Fay Weldon. London: Orion, 1992, pp.1-308.

105. Dingle: Brandon, 1992. 352p.

106. London: Penguin (Penguin Film and TV Tie-In Edition), 1992. 449p.

107. New York: Tor, 1992. 384p.

108. "Trad. de l'Anglais par Lucienne Molitor". Paris: J'ai lu, 1992. 505p. [French language edition]

109. Paris: Pockot, 1992. [French language edition]

110. *Drácula*. Barcelona: Ultramar, 1992. 398p. [Spanish language edition]

111. "Traducion de Arturo Del Rio". Buenos Aires: Editorial Leviatan, 1992. [Spanish language edition]

112. "Aus d. Engl. von Stasi Kull". München: Hanser, 1992. 526p. [German language edition]

113. *Horror Classics. Three Novels in One Volume. Terrifying Novels, Sensational Films. Dracula, Frankenstein* and *The Strange Case of Dr Jekyll and Mr Hyde*. London: Chancellor, 1993, pp.8-316.

114. Ware: Wordsworth, 1993. 335p.

115. Oxford: ISIS (ISIS Classics), 1993. 479p. [Large print edition]

116. Edited and with an Introduction by Maurice Hindle. Harmondsworth: Penguin, 1993. 520p.

117. Edited by Marjory Howes. London: Dent (Everyman's Library), 1993, 398p.

118. *The Essential Dracula, The Definitive Annotated Edition of Bram Stoker's Classic Novel*, "written and edited by Leonard Wolf. Notes, Bibliography and Filmography Revised in Collaboration with Roxanna Stuart. Illustrated by Christopher Bing". New York: Plume/Penguin USA, 1993. 484p

119. *Dracula. Roman.* München: Goldmann, 1993. 528p. [German language edition]

120. *Dracula. Roman.* München: Bastei Lübbe, 1993. [German language edition]

121. *Dracula - roman.* "Traduit de l'Anglais par Lucienne Molitor". Paris: Marabout, 1993. [French language edition]

122. *Drácula*, translated and edited by Juan Antonio Molina Foix. Madrid: Cátedra, 1993. 630p. [Spanish language edition]

123. *Drácula*, translated by Francisco Torres Oliver. Barcelona: Bruguera (Círculo de Lectores), 1993. 493p. [Spanish language edition]

124. *Drakula*, translated and edited by Iñaki Mendiguren, illustrated by Jos Mari Ortizé. Donostia: Elkar, 1993. 70p. [Abridged Basque language edition]

125. London: Penguin (Penguin Popular Classics), 1994. 449p.

126. "Large Type Edition". New York: G.K. Hall, 1994. 592p.

127. *Dracula*, "Aus d. Engl. von Wulf H. Bergner". [München]: Moewig bei Ullstein, 1994. 304p. [German language edition]

128. "The Death of Dracula" [i.e., extract from "Chapter 27"], rpt in Ornella Volta and Valeria Riva eds., *The Vampire, Presented by Roger Vadim*, London: Pan Books, 1965, pp.304-13.

129. "Dracula" [i.e., extracts from "Chapter 1" and "Chapter 3"], rpt in Christopher Frayling ed., *Vampyres, Lord Byron to Count Dracula*, London: Faber and Faber, 1991, pp.364-83.

Miss Betty

130. **Miss Betty** by Bram Stoker. London: C. Arthur Pearson (Latter Day Stories), 1898. 202p.

131. London: C. Arthur Pearson (Pearson's 6d Novels, number 209), n.d. [1913]. 118p.

132. "First New English Library Edition". London: New English Library, 1974. 160p.

The Mystery of the Sea

133. **The Mystery of the Sea**. A Novel by Bram Stoker, Author of "Dracula". New York: Doubleday, Page, 1902. 498p.

134. London: William Heinemann, 1902. 498p.

135. London: William Heinemann, 1902. 454p. [Abridged edition]

136. London: William Heinemann (Heinemann's Colonial Library, number 243) 1902. 498p.

137. 2 Volumes. Leipzig: Heinemann and Balasteir (The English Library, Volumes 211-2), 1903.

138. "Popular Edition". London: William Rider, 1913. 498p.

139. "New Edition". London: William Rider 1922. 498p.

140. "Cheap Edition". London: William Rider, n.d. [1929]. 318p. [Abridged edition]

141. "The Seer" [i.e., "Chapter One"], rpt in Peter Haining ed., *Shades of Dracula. Bram Stoker's Uncollected Stories*, London: William Kimber, 1982, pp.123-33.

The Jewel of Seven Stars

142. **The Jewel of Seven Stars** by Bram Stoker, Author of "The Mystery of the Sea", "Dracula", "The Snake's Pass", "The Watter's Mou'", etc.. London: William Heinemann, 1903. 337p.

143. London: William Heinemann (Heinemann's Colonial Library, number 276), 1903. 337p.

144. "By Bram Stoker, Author of *Dracula*, etc.". New York and London: Harper, 1904. 311p.

145. New York: W.R. Caldwell (Three Owls Edition, The International Adventure Library), 1904. 310p.

146. New York: Harper, 1923. 311p.

147. London: William Rider, 1912. 307p. [Abridged edition]

148. London: William Rider, 1919. 307p. [Abridged edition]

149. London: Arrow, 1962. 254p. [Abridged edition]

150. London: Jarrolds, 1966. 254p. [Abridged edition]

151. Rpt in *Dracula's Curse and The Jewel of Seven Stars*. New York: Tower, 1968, pp.21-218.

152. Leicester: Ulverscroft, 1967. 234p. [Abridged large print edition]

153. New York: Scholastic Book Services, 1972. 301p. [Abridged by Ann Reit]

154. North Hollywood: Fantasy House, 1974.

155. London: Arrow, 1975. 254p. [Abridged edition]

156. New Haven CT: Leete's Island, 1978. 310p.

157. *La joya de las siete estrellas*, translated by Isaac García. Barcelona: Forum, 1984. [Spanish language edition]

158. *La joya de las siete estrellas*, translated by Javier Gomez Monpou. Barcelona: Montesinos, 1987. [Spanish language edition]

159. New York: Carroll and Graf, 1989. 254p.

160. Stroud: Alan Sutton, 1996. 178p.

161. "Introduced by David Glover". Oxford: Oxford University Press (Oxford Popular Fiction), 1996. 214p. [Includes unabridged and revised versions of the concluding chapter]

162. "Annotated and edited by Clive Leatherdale". Westcliff-on-Sea: Desert Island, 1996. 256p. [Includes unabridged and revised versions of the concluding chapter]

163. "The Bridal of Death" [i.e. "Powers — Old and New" (Chapter 16) and the conclusion from "The Great Experiment" (Chapter 20) of the First Edition], rpt in Peter Haining ed., *Midnight Tales*, London: Peter Owen, 1990, pp.151-82.

The Man

164. **The Man**, by Bram Stoker. London: William Heinemann, 1905. 436p.

165. London: William Heinemann (Heinemann's Colonial Library, number 319), 1905. 436p.

166. *The Gates of Life* by Bram Stoker, Author of "Dracula", "Miss Betty", "The Jewel of Seven Stars", etc., with Illustrations by F.B. Ma Dan. New York: Cupples and Leon, 1908. 332p. [Abridged by the Author]

167. London: Robert Hayes (Popular 2 Shilling Novel Series, number 4), n.d. [c.1920?]. 253p. [Abridged edition]

Lady Athlyne

168. **Lady Athlyne** by Bram Stoker, Author of "Dracula", "The Man", etc.. London: William Heinemann, 1908. 333p.

169. London: William Heinemann (Heinemann's Colonial Library), 1908. 333p.

170. New York: P.R. Reynolds, n.d. [1908?]. 333p.

171. New York: Frank Lovell, 1909.

The Lady of the Shroud

172. **The Lady of the Shroud** by Bram Stoker, Author of "Dracula", "Lady Athlyne", etc.. London: William Heinemann, 1909. 367p.

173. London: William Heinemann (Heinemann's Colonial Library), 1909. 367p.

174. London: William Rider, 1914. 355p.

175. London: William Rider, 1920. 362p.

176. London: William Rider, 1925. 355p.

177. "Twentieth Edition". London: William Rider, 1934. 316p.

178. London: Arrow, 1962. 192p [Abridged edition]

179. London: Jarrolds, 1966. 192p. [Abridged edition]

180. New York: Paperback Library (Paperback Library Gothic), 1966. 288p.

181. London: Arrow, 1974. 192p. [Abridged edition]

182.   Stroud: Alan Sutton/University of Luton, 1994. 258p.

183.   Dover NH: Alan Sutton, 1994. 258p.

The Lair of the White Worm

184.   **The Lair of the White Worm**, by Bram Stoker, Author of "Dracula", etc..
London: William Rider, 1911. 328p. [With six colour illustrations by
Pamela Colman Smith]

185.   London: W. Foulsham, n.d.. [1925]. 190p. [Abridged edition]

186.   London: W. Foulsham (The Mayflower Library, number 8), n.d. [1945].
190p. [Abridged edition]

187.   London: Arrow, 1960. 191p. [Abridged edition]

188.   London: Jarrolds, 1966. 191p. [Abridged edition]

189.   *The Garden of Evil.* New York: Paperback Library, 1966. 220p.

190.   *The Garden of Evil.* New York: Paperback Library, 1969, 220p.

191.   *Le Repaire du Ver Blanc.* Traduction de François Truchaud. Paris: Christian
Bourgeois Editeur, 1970. [French language edition]

192.   London: Arrow, 1974. 191p. [Abridged edition]

193.   New York: Kensington (Zebra Books), 1979. 191p. [Abridged edition]

194.   London: Target (A Target Classic), 1981. 156p. [Abridged edition]

195.   *La madriguera del gusano blanco,* translated by J.A. Molina Foix.
Barcelona: Forum, 1984. [Spanish language edition]

196.   London: Target, 1986, 156p. [Abridged edition]

197.   *A Bram Stoker Omnibus Edition. Dracula and The Lair of the White Worm.
Complete and Unabridged, with new original material.* Introduction by
Richard Dalby. London: Foulsham, 1986, pp.333-511.

198.   London: W.H. Allen, 1986. 156p. [Abridged edition]

199. *La guarida del gusano blanco*, translated by Ramon Castelotte. Madrid: Miraguano, 1988. [Spanish language edition]

200. Dingle: Brandon, 1991, 192p. [Abridged edition]

201. *El catau del cuc blanc*, translated by Carme Geronès. Barcelona: Laertes, 1991. [Catalan language edition]

202. *Bram Stoker's Dracula Omnibus. Dracula, The Lair of the White Worm, Dracula's Guest*. Introduction by Fay Weldon. London: Orion, 1992, pp.309-426. [Abridged edition]

ii. Collections of Stories

Under the Sunset

Contents: "Under the Sunset", "The Rose Prince", "The Invisible Giant", "The Shadow Builder", "How 7 Went Mad", "Lies and Lilies", "The Castle of the King", "The Wondrous Child".

203. **Under the Sunset** By Bram Stoker M.A., with [33] illustrations by W. Fitzgerald and W.V. Cockburn. London: Sampson Low, Marston, Searle and Rivington, 1882 [Published Nov 1881]. 190p.

204. "Second Edition", with [48] illustrations by W. Fitzgerald and W.V. Cockburn. London: Sampson Low, Marston, Searle and Rivington, 1882. 191p.

205. "First American Edition", edited by R. Reginald and Douglas Menville. North Hollywood, California: Newcastle (Newcastle Forgotten Fantasy Library, Volume 17), 1978. 190p.

206. San Bernardino, California: R. Reginald (The Borgo Press), 1990. 190p.

207. *Bram Stoker's "Under the Sunset": An Edition With Introductory, Biographical and Critical Material* by Douglas Oliver Street. A Dissertation Presented to the Faculty of the Graduate College in the University of Nebraska, May 1977. Ann Arbor: University Microfilms International, 1978. [Xerox transparency, number 77-23,161]

208. "The Invisible Giant", rpt in Charles Osborne ed., *The Bram Stoker Bedside Companion*, London: Victor Gollancz, 1973, pp.42-55.

209. "The Spectre of Doom" [i.e. "The Invisible Giant"], rpt in Peter Haining ed., *Midnight Tales*, London: Peter Owen, 1990, pp.30-43.

210. "The Castle of the King", rpt in Peter Haining ed., *Shades of Dracula. Bram Stoker's Uncollected Stories*, London: William Kimber, 1982, pp.74-90.

211. "The Castle of the King", rpt in Marvyn Kaye and Saralee Kaye eds., *A Classic Collection of Haunting Ghost Stories*, London: Warner, 1994, pp.253-66.

Snowbound. The Record of a Theatrical Touring Party

Contents: "The Occasion", "A Lesson In Pets", "Coggins's Property", "The Slim Syrens", "A New Departure in Art", "Mick the Devil", "In Fear of Death", "At Last", "Chin Music", "A Deputy Waiter", "Work'us", "A Corner in Dwarfs", "A Criminal Star", "A Star Trap", "A Moonlight Effect".

212. **Snowbound. The Record of a Theatrical Touring Party**, by Bram Stoker. London: Collier (Collier's Shilling Library), 1908. 256p.

213. "At Last", rpt in Peter Haining ed., *Shades of Dracula. Bram Stoker's Uncollected Stories*, London: William Kimber, 1982, pp.189-97.

214. "A Criminal Star", rpt in Peter Haining ed., *Midnight Tales*, London: Peter Owen, 1990, pp.143-50.

215. "A Star Trap", rpt in Charles Osborne ed., *The Bram Stoker Bedside Companion*, London: Victor Gollancz, 1973, pp.102-14.

216. "Death in the Wings" [i.e. "A Star Trap"], rpt in Peter Haining ed., *Midnight Tales*, London: Peter Owen, 1990, pp.59-70.

Contents: "Dracula's Guest", "The Judge's House", "The Squaw", "The Secret of the Growing Gold", "A Gipsy Prophecy", "The Coming of Abel Behenna", "The Burial of the Rats", "A Dream of Red Hands", "Crooken Sands".

217. **Dracula's Guest and Other Weird Stories** by Bram Stoker, Author of "Dracula", "The Mystery of the Sea", "The Jewel of Seven Stars", "The Lady of the Shroud", etc., etc.. London: George Routledge, 1914. 200p.

218. "Prince of Wales' Theatre Souvenir Edition". London: Prince of Wales' Theatre, 1927. 200p. [A limited edition of 1,000 copies, commemorating the 250th London Performance of Hamilton Deane's stage adaptation of *Dracula* on 14 Sept 1927]

219. New York: Hillman-Curl (A Clue Club Mystery), 1937. 284p.

220. [Toronto]: McLeod, 1938.

221. London: Jarrolds, 1966. 192p.

222. London: Arrow, 1966. 192p.

223. London: Arrow, 1974. 192p.

224. *Draculas Gast: 6 Gruselgeschichten*, "Aus d. Engl. von Erich Fivian, Zeichn. von Peter Neugebauer". Zürich: Diogenes Verl. (Diogenes Taschenbuch 20135), 1974. 135p. [German language edition]

225. New York: Kensington (Zebra Books), 1978. 192p.

226. *El invitado de Drácula y otros relatos fantásticos*, translated by E.M. Fariñas. Barcelona: Producciones Editoriales, 1980. 244p. [Spanish language edition]

227. Dingle: Brandon, 1990. 160p.

228. *Bram Stoker's Dracula Omnibus, Dracula, The Lair of the White Worm, Dracula's Guest.* "Introduction" by Fay Weldon. London: Orion, 1992, pp.427-543.

229. *L'Invité de Dracula.* Paris: UGE, 1992. [French language edition]

230. *Draculas Gast*: "Erzälhungen Aus d. Engl. von Erich Fivian und H. Haas, Zeichn. von Peter Neugebauer". Zürich: Diogenes Verl., 1993. 144p. [German language edition]

231. "Dracula's Guest", rpt in *Fifty Years of Ghost Stories*, London: Hutchinson, 1935, pp.401-12.

232. "Dracula's Curse" [i.e. "Dracula's Guest"], rpt in *Dracula's Curse and The Jewel of Seven Stars*, New York: Tower, 1968, pp.1-20.

233. "El invitado de Drácula" [i.e., "Dracula's Guest"], rpt in Forrest J. Ackerman ed., *Las mejores historias de horror*, translated by Miguel Giménez. Barcelona: Bruguera (Libro amigo), 1969, pp.65-79. [Spanish language edition, rpt 1970, 1971 (twice), 1972, 1973, 1974]

234. "Dracula's Guest", rpt in James Dickie ed., *The Undead. Vampire Masterpieces*, London: Neville Spearman, 1971, pp.27-40.

235. "Dracula's Guest", rpt in Charles Osborne ed., *The Bram Stoker Bedside Companion*, London: Victor Gollancz, 1973, pp.29-41.

236. "Dracula's Guest", rpt in James Dickie ed., *The Undead, Vampire Masterpieces*, London: Pan, 1973, pp.27-40.

237. "Walpurgis Night" [i.e., "Dracula's Guest"], rpt in Peter Haining ed., *Shades of Dracula. Bram Stoker's Uncollected Stories*, London: William Kimber, 1982, pp.109-22.

238. "Dracula's Guest", rpt in Peter Haining ed., *Vampire. Chilling Tales of the Undead*, London: Target, 1985, pp.32-45.

239. "The Dream in the Dead House" [i.e. "Dracula's Guest"], rpt in Peter Haining ed., *Midnight Tales*, London: Peter Owen, 1990, pp.17-29.

240. "Dracula's Guest", rpt in Alan Ryan ed., *The Penguin Book of Vampire Stories, Two Centuries of Great Stories with a Bite*, London: Penguin, 1988, pp.163-74.

241. "Dracula's Guest", rpt in *Great Vampires and Other Horrors*, London: Chancellor, 1992, pp.50-9.

242. "El invitado del Drácula" [i.e., "Dracula's Guest"], translated by Francisco Torres Oliver, rpt in *Vampiros*, Madrid: Siruela, 1992. [Spanish language edition]

243. "Dracula's Daughter" [i.e., "Dracula's Guest"], rpt in Peter Haining ed., *The Ghouls*, London: Chancellor, 1994, pp.167-78.

244. "The Judge's House", rpt in Montague Summers ed., *The Supernatural Omnibus*, London: Victor Gollancz, 1931, pp.78-95

245. "The Judge's House", rpt in Herbert van Thal ed., *The Second Pan Book of Horror Stories*, London: Pan, 1960, pp.107-28.

246. "La casa del juez" [i.e., "The Judge's House"], rpt in Rafael Llopis Paret ed., *Cuentos de Terror*, Madrid: Taurus, 1963. [Spanish language edition]

247. "The Judge's House", rpt in Montague Summers ed., *The Supernatural Omnibus*, 2 vols, London: Panther, 1967, Vol 1, pp.48-64.

248. "The Judge's House", rpt in Charles Osborne ed., *The Bram Stoker Bedside Companion, London*: Victor Gollancz, 1973, pp.56-75.

249. "La casa del juez" [i.e., "The Judge's House"] rpt in A. Van Hageland ed., *Las mejores historias de ultratumba*, translated by F. Corripio. Barcelona: Bruguera (Libro amigo), 1973, pp.255-79. [Spanish language edition, rpt 1974, 1975]

250. "The Judge's House", rpt in Montague Summers ed., *The Supernatural Omnibus*, London: Victor Gollancz, 1974, pp.78-95.

251. "The Judge's House", rpt in Stephanie Dowrick ed., *Classic Tales of Horror*, London: Book Club Associates, 1976, pp.136-53.

252. "The Judge's House", rpt in Leslie Shepard ed., *The Dracula Book of Classic Horror Stories*, London: Robert Hale, 1992, pp.151-69.

253. "The Judge's House", rpt in Montague Summers ed., *The Supernatural Omnibus*, London: Bracken, 1994, pp.78-95.

254. "The Squaw", rpt in *A Century of Thrillers*, Second Series, London: Daily Express, 1935, pp.353-64.

255. "The Squaw", rpt in J.M. Parrish and John R. Crossland eds., *The Mammoth Book of Thrillers, Ghosts and Mysteries*, London: Odhams, 1936, pp.743-54.

256. "The Squaw", rpt in Dorothy L. Sayers ed., *Great Stories of Detection, Mystery and Horror*, London: Victor Gollancz, 1928, pp.1099-110.

257. "The Squaw", rpt in Dorothy L. Sayers ed., *Great Stories of Detection, Mystery and Horror*, 2 Vols, London: Victor Gollancz, 1947, Vol 2, "Mystery and Horror", pp.489-500.

258. "The Squaw", rpt in Charles Osborne ed., *The Bram Stoker Bedside Companion*, London: Victor Gollancz, 1973, pp.115-27.

259. "The Squaw", rpt in Peter Haining ed., *Midnight Tales*, London: Peter Owen, 1990, pp.85-97.

260. "The Squaw", rpt in *Horror by Lamplight*, London: Chancellor, 1993, pp.261-9.

261. "The Secret of the Growing Gold", rpt in Charles Osborne ed., *The Bram Stoker Bedside Companion*, London: Victor Gollancz, 1973, pp.15-28.

262. "The Secret of the Growing Gold", rpt in Mary Danby ed., *The Twelfth Fontana Book of Horror Stories*, Glasgow: Collins/Fontana, 1979, pp.30-44.

263. "The Burial of the Rats", rpt in Charles Osborne ed., *The Bram Stoker Bedside Companion*, London: Victor Gollancz, 1973, pp.76-101.

264. "The Burial of the Rats", rpt in Peter Haining ed., *Christopher Lee's New Chamber of Horrors*, St. Alban's: Mayflower, 1974, pp.64-92.

265. "Crooken Sands", rpt in Charles Osborne ed., *The Bram Stoker Bedside Companion*, London: Victor Gollancz, 1973, pp.128-50.

iii. Dramatic Works

Dracula, or the Un-Dead, in a Prologue and Five Acts

266. **Dracula or, the Un-Dead in a Prologue and Five Acts**. London: Royal Lyceum Theatre, 1897.

Miss Betty. A Play in Four Acts

267. **Miss Betty. A Play in Four Acts**. London: Royal Lyceum Theatre, 1898.

268. **The Mystery of the Sea. A Drama, in a Prologue and Five Acts**.
London: Royal Lyceum Theatre, 1902.

Fiction in Collaboration

The Fate of Fenella. Contents: "Fenella", Helen Mathers; "Kisme", Justin
Mccarthy; "How it Strikes a Contemporary", Francis Eleanor Trollope; "Between
Two Fires", Arthur Conan Doyle; "Complications", Mary Crommelin; "A Woman's
View of the Matter", F.C. Phillips; "So Near - So Far Away", "Rita" [Pseud.];
"The Tragedy", Joseph Hatton; "Free Once Again", Mrs. Lovett Cameron; "Lord
Castleton Explains", Bram Stoker; "Madame De Vigny's Revenge", Florence
Marryat; "To Live or Die", Frank Danby; "The Scars Remained", Mrs. Edward
Kennard; "Derelict", Richard Dowling; "Another Rift", Mrs. Hungerford; "In New
York", Arthur A'Beckett; "Confined in a Madhouse", Jean Middlemass; "Within
Sight of Home", Clement Scott; "A Vision From the Sea", Clo Graves; "Through
Fire and Water", H.W. Lucy; "Alive or Dead?", Adeline Sergeant; "Retribution",
George Manville Fenn; "Sick Unto Death", "Tasma" [Pseud.]; "Whom the Gods
Hate Die Hard", F. Anstey.

269. "Chapter X" of "The Fate of Fenella", *The Gentlewoman* 4 (1892): 138-9.

270. "Lord Castleton Explains", [i.e., "Chapter X"], rpt in John Seymour ed., *The
Fate of Fenella, A Novel*, Leipzig: Tauchnitz, 1892.

271. "Lord Castleton Explains", [i.e., "Chapter X"], rpt in J.S. Wood ed., *The
Fate of Fenella*, by twenty-four well-known authors, with seventy
illustrations, "Third and cheaper edition", London: Hutchinson, 1892.

272. "The Fate of Fenella", [i.e., "Chapter X"], rpt in Peter Haining ed., *Shades
of Dracula. Bram Stoker's Uncollected Stories*, London: William Kimber,
1982, pp.91-100.

273. "A Deed of Vengeance?" [i.e., "Chapter X"], rpt in Peter Haining ed.,
Midnight Tales, London: Peter Owen, 1990, pp.98-106.

The Necessity for Political Honesty

274. **The Necessity for Political Honesty.** University of Dublin, College Historical Society. Address Delivered in the Dining Hall of Trinity College at the First Meeting of the Twenty-Eighth Session, on Wednesday Evening, November 13, 1872, by the Auditor, Abraham Stoker A.B.. Dublin: James Charles, 1872. 32p.

The Duties of Clerks of Petty Sessions in Ireland

275. **The Duties of Clerks of Petty Sessions in Ireland** by Bram Stoker M.A., Inspector of Petty Sessions. Published by Authority. Dublin: Printed for the Author by John Falconer, 1879. 248p.

A Glimpse of America

276. **A Glimpse of America.** A Lecture Given at the London Institution, 28th December 1885, by Bram Stoker M.A.. London: Sampson Low, Marston, 1886. 48p.

Sir Henry Irving and Miss Ellen Terry in Robespierre, Merchant of Venice, The Bells, Nance Oldfield, The Amber Heart, Waterloo, etc.

277. **Sir Henry Irving and Miss Ellen Terry in "Robespierre", "Merchant of Venice", "The Bells", "Nance Oldfield", "The Amber Heart", "Waterloo", etc..** Drawn by Pamela C. Smith. New York: Doubleday and McClure, 1899. 12p.

Personal Reminiscences of Henry Irving

278. **Personal Reminiscences of Henry Irving** by Bram Stoker. London: William Heinemann, 1906. Two Vols. 372p & 388p.

279. New York: Macmillan, 1906. 2 Vols. 372p & 338p.

280. "Revised and Cheaper Edition". London: William Heinemann, 1907. 480p.

281. Westport CT: Greenwood, 1970. 2 Vols. 372p & 388p.

282. "Midnight Tales" [adapted from stories embedded in *Personal Reminiscences of Henry Irving*, 1906] comprising "The Funeral Party" (i.e., Vol. 1, pp.347-9), "The Shakespeare Mystery" [not traced], "A Deal with the Devil" (i.e. Vol. 2, p.76), rpt in Peter Haining ed., *Midnight Tales*, London: Peter Owen, 1990, pp.137-42.

Famous Imposters

283. **Famous Imposters**. With Ten Illustrations. London: Sidgwick & Jackson, 1910. 349p.

284. New York: Sturgis and Walton, 1910. 349p.

285. London: The Library Association, 1967. 349p.

Fiction in Periodicals and Anthologies

286. "The Crystal Cup" by Abraham Stoker, *London Society* 22 (1872): 228-35.

287. "The Crystal Cup", rpt in George Locke ed., *The Land of the Unseen: Lost Supernatural Stories 1828-1902*, [New York]: Ferret Fantasy, 1973, pp.51-61.

288. "The Crystal Cup", rpt in Peter Haining ed., *Shades of Dracula. Bram Stoker's Uncollected Stories*, London: William Kimber, 1982, pp.14-28.

289. "The Primrose Path. A Serial in Ten Chapters" by A. Stoker, Esq., *The Shamrock* 12 (1875): 289-93; 312-7; 330-4; 345-9; 360-5.

290. "Buried Treasures. A Serial in Four Chapters" by A. Stoker, Esq., *The Shamrock* 12 (1875): 376-9; 403-6.

291. "The Chain of Destiny. A Serial in Four Parts" by A. Stoker, Esq., *The Shamrock* 12 (1875): 446-9; 498-9; 514-6; 530-3; 546-8.

292. "The Chain of Destiny", rpt in P. Haining ed., *Shades of Dracula, Bram Stoker's Uncollected Stories*, London: William Kimber, 1982, pp.29-73.

293. "Our New House", *The Theatre Annual for 1886*: 71-8.

294. "The Dualitists; or, the Death Doom of the Double Born", *The Theatre Annual for 1887*: 18-29.

295. *The Dualitists; or, the Death Doom of the Double Born.* "Edition limited to 125 copies, of which 100 are for sale, set in Barbou type and printed on Ingres D'Arches paper." Introduction by Richard Dalby. Edinburgh: Tragara, 1986.

296. "The Dualitists; or, the Death Doom of the Double Born", rpt in Peter Haining ed., *Midnight Tales*, London: Peter Owen, 1990, pp.44-58.

297. "The Judge's House", *The Illustrated Sporting and Dramatic News*, Christmas Number ("Holly Leaves"), 5 Dec 1891: 10-1.

298. "The Secret of the Growing Gold", *Black and White* 3, 23 Jan 1892: 118-21.

299. "The Squaw", *The Illustrated Sporting and Dramatic News*, Christmas Number ("Holly Leaves"), 2 Dec 1893: 24-5.

300. "A Dream of Red Hands" ("A Novel in a Nutshell"), *The Sketch* 6 (1894): 578-80.

301. "The Red Stockade: A Story Told by the Old Coastguard", *Cosmopolitan Magazine* 17 (1894): 619-30.

302. "The Red Stockade: A Story Told by the Old Coastguard", rpt in Peter Haining ed., *Midnight Tales*, London: Peter Owen, 1990, pp.120-36.

303. "The 'Eroes of the Thames: The Story of a Frustrated Advertisement", *The Royal Magazine*, Oct 1908: 566-70.

304. "The 'Eroes of the Thames: The Story of a Frustrated Advertisement", *The Bram Stoker Society Journal* 2 (1990): 24-33.

305. "The Way of Peace", *Everybody's Story Magazine*, Dec 1909: 204-9.

306. "The Way of Peace. A story of quiet Irish humour and tenderness, about the happiest couple in the country, and the secret of it", rpt in *The Bram Stoker Society Journal* 1 (1989): 34-41.

307. "In the Valley of the Shadow", rpt in Peter Haining ed., *Shades of Dracula. Bram Stoker's Uncollected Stories*, London: William Kimber, 1982, pp.198-204.

308. "Greater Love", *The London Magazine* 33 (1914-5): 161-8.

Poetry

309. "The One Thing Needful", in *A Volunteer Haversack*, Edinburgh: Printed for the Queen's Rifle Volunteer Brigade: the Royal Scots, Edinburgh, 1902, pp.173-4.

310. "The One Thing Needful", rpt in *The Queen's Carol, An Anthology of Poems, Stories, Essays, Drawings and Music by British Authors, Artists, and Composers*, London, Manchester and Paris: Daily Mail, 1905, p.105.

311. "The One Thing Needful", rpt in Richard Dalby, *Bram Stoker. A Bibliography of First Editions*, London: Dracula, 1983, p.79.

Interviews and Journalism.

312. Untitled account of the "University Night" performance of *Hamlet* given by Henry Irving at the Theatre Royal, Dublin, on 11 Dec 1876. Written for *The Dublin Mail* and originally printed c.12 Dec 1876, rpt in Bram Stoker, *Personal Reminiscences of Henry Irving*, London: William Heinemann, 1906, 2 Vols., Vol. 1, pp.37-40.

313. "Address to Henry Irving, Esq., presented by the Graduates and Undergraduates of Trinity College, Dublin [11 Dec 1876]" rpt in Austin Brereton, *Henry Irving: A Biographical Sketch*, London: David Bogue, 1883, pp.55-6.

314. Henry Irving [i.e., Bram Stoker], "The American Audience", *The Fortnightly Review* New Series 37 (1885): 197-201.

315. "Actor-Managers", *The Nineteenth Century* 27 (June 1890): 1040-51.

316. "Dramatic Criticism", *North American Review* 158 (Mar 1894): 325-31.

317.   "The Art of Ellen Terry", *The Playgoer* 1 (Oct 1901): 39-48.

318.   "Introduction" to Hall Caine, *The Deemster*, London: Eveleigh Nash and Grayson, 1905, pp.v-vi.

319.   "Fifty Years on the Stage. An Appreciation of Miss Ellen Terry by Bram Stoker", *The Graphic*, 28 April 1906: 537.

320.   "Fifty Years on the Stage. An Appreciation of Miss Ellen Terry by Bram Stoker", rpt in *The Bram Stoker Society Journal* 1 (1989): 24-6.

321.   "The Great White Fair in Dublin: How there has arisen on the site of the old Donnybrook Fair a great Exhibition as typical of the New Ireland as the former festival was of the Ireland of the Past", *The World's Work* "Special Irish Edition" 9 (May 1907): 570-6.

322.   "The World's Greatest Ship-Building Yard. Impressions of a Visit to Messrs. Harland and Wolff's Ship-Building Yards at Belfast", *The World's Work* "Special Irish Edition" 9 (May 1907): 647-50.

323.   "Sir Arthur Conan Doyle Tells of His Career and Work, His Sentiments Towards America, and His Approaching Marriage", *The World* [New York], 28 July 1907: 8.

324.   "The Tendency of the Modern Stage. A Talk With Sir W.S. Gilbert on Things Theatrical", *The Daily Chronicle*, 2 Jan 1908: 8.

325.   "The Tendency of the Modern Stage. A Talk with Sir W.S. Gilbert on Things Theatrical", rpt in *The Bram Stoker Society Journal* 3 (1991): 38-45

326.   "Mr Winston Churchill talks of his Hopes, His Work, and His Ideals to Bram Stoker", *The Daily Chronicle*, 15 Jan 1908: 8.

327.   "Mr Winston Churchill talks of his Hopes, His Work, and His Ideals to Bram Stoker", rpt in *The Bram Stoker Society Journal* 2 (1990): 38-45.

328.   "Sir Arthur Conan Doyle Tells of his Work and Career", *The Daily Chronicle*, 14 Feb 1908: 8.

329.   "How Mr Pinero Writes Plays, Told in an Interview by Bram Stoker", *The Daily Chronicle*, 15 Feb 1908: 8.

330.   "The Question of a National Theatre", *The Nineteenth Century* 63 (May 1908): 734-42.

331. "Mr DeMorgan's Habits of Work. The Career of a Man Who Began to Write After He Was Sixty-Four Years Old", *The World's Work* (United States Edition) 16 (July 1908): 10337-42.

332. "The Work of William DeMorgan. An Artist, Manufacturer, and Inventor Who Began Writing Novels at the Age of Sixty-Four", *The World's Work* 12 (1908): 160-4.

333. "The Censorship of Fiction", *The Nineteenth Century and After* 64 (Sept 1908): 479-87.

334. "The Censorship of Fiction" [Extract], rpt in Harold Bloom ed., *Classic Horror Writers*, New York: Chelsea House, 1994, pp.154-5.

335. "Americans as Actors", *Fortnightly Review* 91 (Feb 1909): 243-52.

336. "Dead-Heads", *Fortnightly Review* 92 (Oct 1909): 646-58.

337. "The American 'Tramp' Question and the Old English Vagrancy Laws", *North American Review* 190 (1909): 605-14.

338. "The Censorship of Stage Plays", *The Nineteenth Century and After* 66 (Dec 1909): 974-89.

339. "Irving and Stage Lighting", *The Nineteenth Century and After* 69 (May 1911): 903-12.

Manuscript Material

340. **The Bodleian Library, Oxford.**

Letter from Bram Stoker to A.E. Parry, 1903.

Fifteen letters from Sidgwick and Jackson, Publishers, to Bram Stoker, 1910-1911.

Two Letters from Sidgwick and Jackson, Publishers, to Florence Stoker, 1912.

341. **The British Library, London.**

Letter from Bram Stoker to T.H.S. Escott, 1883.

Letter from Bram Stoker to A. Garner, 1889.

Two Letters from Bram Stoker to Cassell and Company, 1889.

Letter from Bram Stoker to W.E. Gladstone, 1897.

Note from Bram Stoker to Mr MacNaghten, 1897.

Letter from Bram Stoker to Bernard Shaw, 1898.

Two Letters from Bram Stoker to Lord Avebury, 1907.

Two Letters from Bram Stoker to the Royal Literary Fund, 1911.

Correspondence of Bram Stoker in the Archive of the Society of Authors.

342. **The Brotherton Collection, University of Leeds.**

The Collected In-Mail of Bram Stoker, c.1880-c.1910.

Personal Impressions of America [sic], bound with newspaper cuttings describing the lecture.

The Secret of the Growing Gold [1891], short story, 1 vol.

Seven Golden Buttons [i.e., *Miss Betty*]. Novella, 1 vol.

343. **Colby College, Maine.**

Letter from Thomas Hardy to Bram Stoker, c.1908.

344. **The Garrick Club, London.**

Eleven Letters and a telegram from Bram Stoker to Percy Fitzgerald, 1906.

345. **Hove Central Library, Sussex.**

Letter from Bram Stoker to Frank J. Arlton, 1905.

346. **The University of Illinois at Urbana-Champaign.**

Letter from W.G. Wills to Bram Stoker, undated.

347. **University of Newcastle-Upon-Tyne.**

Letter from Bram Stoker to Frederic Whyte, undated.

348. **University of Nottingham.**

Two Letters from Bram Stoker to R. Warwick Bond, 1896.

349. **University of Reading.**

Letter from Bram Stoker in the Archive of George Bell and Sons, 1903.

350. **Richmond Central Library.**

Letter from Bram Stoker in the Correspondence Files of Douglas Sladen, undated.

351. **The Rosenbach Museum and Library, Philadelphia.**

The working notes for *Dracula*, dated from 8 Mar 1890. [These are summarised in "Bram Stoker's Working Papers for Dracula", Christopher Frayling ed., *Vampyres, From Lord Byron to Count Dracula*, London: Faber and Faber, 1991, pp.303-31.]

352. **The National Library of Scotland, Edinburgh.**

Letter from Bram Stoker to J.H. Balfour Brown, 1889.

Letter from Bram Stoker in the Correspondence Files of Clement K. Shorter and John Malcolm Bulloch, 1897.

353. **The Shakespeare Birthplace Trust, Shakespeare Centre Library, Stratford-Upon-Avon.**

The Papers of Henry Irving and Ellen Terry from the Bram Stoker Collection. Seventy-seven boxes. Boxes six, seven and eight comprise letters, telegrams and notes by Irving and Stoker, numbered and catalogued in detail.

354. *The Papers of Henry Irving and Ellen Terry from the Bram Stoker Collection, the Shakespeare Centre Library, Stratford-Upon-Avon*, rpt in *Actors and Managers of the English and American Stage*. Series 1. Brighton: Harvester Microform, 1987. 245p. [Printed inventory, accompanied by 30 reels of microfilm]

355. **The Ellen Terry Memorial Museum, Tenterden, Kent.**

Three Letters from Bram Stoker to Ellen Terry, 1891-1906.

356. **The Library of Trinity College, Dublin.**

Famous Imposters, incomplete manuscript, 1910.

Telegram from Bram Stoker, 1907.

357. **University Philosophical Society, Trinity College, Dublin.**

Minute Book completed by Bram Stoker as Secretary of the University Philosophical Society.

Minutes signed by Bram Stoker in the Office of President of the University Philosophical Society.

358. Undated facsimile page in Stoker's hand from the *Minute Book* of the University Philosophical Society, rpt in J.P. Cinnamond ed., *University Philosophical Society, Trinity College Dublin, Centenary Review*, Dublin: The Centenary Committee of the University Philosophical Society, 1953, p.53.

359. **The Victoria and Albert Museum, London**.

Letter from Harry Furniss to Bram Stoker, undated.

360. Facsimile of a letter from Walt Whitman to Bram Stoker dated 6 March, 1876, rpt in Bram Stoker, *Personal Reminiscences of Henry Irving*, London: William Heinemann, 1906, 2 Vols., Vol 2, facing p.97.

361. Correspondence between Bram Stoker and Walt Whitman 1872-1876. Reprinted in: Horace Traubel, ed. Scully Bradley, *With Walt Whitman in Camden, January 21 to April 7, 1889*, Philadelphia: University of Pennsylvania Press, 1953, pp.180-5.

Secondary Bibliography

Contemporary Reviews

Under the Sunset

362. *Notes and Queries*, 12 Nov 1881: 399.

363. *The Spectator* 54 (19 Nov 1881): 1440.

364. *Punch* 81 (3 Dec 1881): 261.

365. *The Academy*, 10 Dec 1881: 431-2.

366. *The Times*, 15 Dec 1881: 11.

The Snake's Pass

367. *Punch* 99 (1890): 269.

368. *The Athenaeum* 96 (20 Dec 1890): 850.

369. *The Publishers' Circular*, 26 Dec 1891: 717.

370. *Harper's Magazine* 82 (3 Feb 1891): Supplement, 488.

The Watter's Mou'

371.   *Punch* 108 (1895): 29.

372.   *The Yorkshire Post*, 9 Jan 1895: 3.

373.   *The Dundee Advertiser*, 10 Jan 1895: 2.

374.   "What to Read", *The Sunday Times*, 13 Jan 1895: 2.

375.   "The Watter's Mou'", *The Morning Post*, 23 Jan 1895: 6.

376.   *The Speaker*, 9 Feb 1895: 166.

377.   *St. James's Gazette*, 12 Feb 1895: 5-6.

378.   *Liverpool Daily Post*, 13 Feb 1895: 6.

379.   *The Athenaeum* 105 (23 Feb 1895): 246.

380.   *St. James's Budget*, 8 Mar 1895: 28.

381.   *The Manchester Guardian*, 19 Mar 1895: 10.

382.   *The Publishers' Weekly* [New York], 14 Sept 1895: 332.

383.   *The Boston Daily Advertiser* [Mass.], 30 Sept 1895: 5

384.   *The Nation*, 27 Feb 1896: 183.

The Shoulder of Shasta

385.   *The Glasgow Herald*, 10 Oct 1895: 10.

386.   *The Daily Telegraph*, 11 Oct 1895: 6.

387.   *Liverpool Daily Post*, 23 Oct 1895: 7.

388.   *The Yorkshire Post*, 24 Oct 1895: 12.

389.   *The Athenaeum* 106 (16 Nov 1895): 677.

390.   *St. James's Gazette*, 16 Nov 1895: 12.

391.   *The Daily Chronicle*, 22 Nov 1895: 3.

392.   *The Spectator*, 22 Feb 1896: 273.

Dracula

393.   *The Bookman* 12 (1897): 129.

394.   *Punch* 112 (1897): 527.

395.   "Mr Bram Stoker's New Story", *Daily News*, 27 May 1897: 6.

396.   *The Daily Mail*, 1 June 1897: 3.

397.   "For Midnight Reading", *Pall Mall Gazette*, 1 June 1897: 11.

398.   "Books of the Day", *The Daily Telegraph*, 3 June 1897: 6.

399.   "Recent Novels", *Morning Post*, 3 June 1897: 2.

400.   "Literature", *North British Daily Mail*, 7 June 1897: 2.

401.   "Publishers' Announcements", *Westminster Gazette*, 10 June 1897: 7.

402.   *The Glasgow Herald*, 10 June 1897: 10.

403.   *The Manchester Guardian*, 15 June 1897: 9.

404.   *The Athenaeum*, 26 June 1897: 835

405.   "The Trail of the Vampire", *St. James's Gazette*, 30 June 1897: 5.

406.   *Saturday Review*, 3 July 1897: 21.

407.   *The Spectator* 79 (31 July 1897): 150-1.

408.   *The Observer*, 1 Aug 1897: 7.

409.   "Chat About Books", *The Daily Mail*, 6 Aug 1897: 3.

410.   *The Publishers' Circular*, 7 Aug 1897: 131.

411. Sub Rosa [i.e., Spencer Leigh Hughes], "Under Cover", *The Gentlewoman*, 21 Aug 1897: 247.

412. "Books of the Day", *The Liverpool Mercury*, 15 Sept 1897: 9.

413. "Recent Works of Fiction", *Springfield Republican* [Mass.], 12 Nov 1899: 15.

414. "The Insanity of the Horrible", *The San Francisco Wave*, 9 Dec 1899: 5.

Miss Betty

415. *The Bookman* [New York] 14 (1898): 21.

416. *Punch* 114 (1898): 105.

417. *The Globe*, 23 Feb 1898: 6.

418. *North British Daily Mail*, 28 Feb 1898: 2.

419. *The Morning Post*, 4 Mar 1898: 3.

420. "Some New Novels", *Daily News*, 21 Mar 1898: 8.

421. *The Athenaeum*, 26 Mar 1898: 401.

422. *The Observer*, 27 Mar 1898: Supplement, 2.

423. Sub Rosa [i.e., Spencer Leigh Hughes], "Under Cover", *The Gentlewoman*, 7 May 1898: 611.

424. *The Bookman* 29 (1905): 38.

The Mystery of the Sea

425. *The Bookman* 23 (1902): 32.

426. *The Dial* 32 (1902): 391.

427. *Punch* 123 (1902): 110.

428. "Bram Stoker's New Romance", *Springfield Republican* [Mass.], 6 April 1902: 19.

429. "Author and Manager", *The Daily Mail*, 18 July 1902: 2.

430. "Second Sight and First Aid", *The Daily Mail*, 5 Aug 1902: 2.

431. *The New York Times*, 13 Sept 1902: 612.

The Jewel of Seven Stars

432. *The Review of Reviews* 28 (1903): 638.

433. *Harper's Weekly* 48 (20 Feb 1904): 276.

434. *The Reader Magazine* [New York] 3 (1904): 657-8.

435. *The New York Times*, 20 May 1923: 19.

436. *The Boston Evening Transcript* [Mass.], 9 June 1923: 5

437. *The Literary Review of the New York Evening Post*, 26 June 1923: 792.

438. *Greensboro Daily News* [N.C.], 26 Aug 1923: 20.

The Man

439. *The Bookman* 29 (1905): 38.

440. *Punch* 129 (1905): 234.

441. "New Novels", *The Manchester Guardian*, 13 Sept 1905: 3.

The Gates of Life

442. Cooper, F.T., "The Gates of Life", *The Bookman* [New York] 28 (1908): 69.

443. *The New York Times*, 15 Aug 1908: 448.

444. *The Nation* 87 (20 Aug 1908): 163.

Personal Reminiscences of Henry Irving

445. *Blackwood's Magazine* 180 (1906): 613.

446. "Sir Henry Irving", *The Bookman* [New York] 24 (1906): 4-6.

447. F.G. Bettany, "Reminiscences of Irving", *The Bookman* 31 (1906): 92-4.

448. *The Academy* 71 (13 Oct 1906): 369.

449. *The New York Times*, 13 Oct 1906: 674.

450. "Irving as Man and Actor", *The Nation* 83 (18 Oct 1906): 334-5.

451. *The Times*, 19 Oct 1906: 353

452. Pyle, Ingram A., "The Intimate Life of Sir Henry Irving", *The Dial* [Chicago], 1 Nov 1906: 276-8.

453. *Outlook* [New York] 84 (26 Nov 1906): 713.

454. *Current Literature* 41 (Dec 1906): 659.

455. *Putnam's Monthly and The Critic* [New York] 1 (Dec 1906): 382.

456. *The Review of Reviews* [New York] 34 (Dec 1906): 757.

457. [Letter], *The New York Times*, 5 Dec 1908: 758.

458. Gilder, Jeanette L., *Putnam's Monthly and The Critic* 1 (Jan 1907): 508.

Lady Athlyne

459. *The Bookman* 34 (1908): 157.

460. *The Athenaeum*, 11 July 1908: 38.

The Lady of the Shroud

461. *The Dundee Advertiser*, 15 July 1909: 2.

462. W.F.P. [i.e., W.F. Purvis], "Bram Stoker's Latest Novel", *The Bookman* 37 (1910): 194.

Famous Imposters

463. *The New York Times*, 8 Oct 1910: 564.

464. *The Bookman* 40 (1911): Supplement, 8.

465. *The Dial* 50 (1911): 97.

466. *Punch* 140 (1911): 144.

467. "The Real Mlle. de Maupin", *The Bookman* [United States Edition], Jan 1911: 456-7.

468. *The Independent* [New York] 70 (12 Jan 1911): 102.

469. *The Spectator*, 28 Jan 1911: 153.

470. *The Athenaeum*, 18 Feb 1911: 184-5.

471. *The New York Times*, 26 Feb 1911: 107.

472. *Literary Digest* [New York] 42 (1 April 1911): 640.

473. *Saturday Review* [London] 3 (1 April 1911): 400.

The Lair of the White Worm

474. *The Times Literary Supplement*, 16 Nov 1911: 466.

475. "Current Literature", *The Daily Telegraph*, 22 Nov 1911: 4.

476. *The Scotsman*, 27 Nov 1911: 2.

477. Anderson, Isaac, *The New York Times*, 9 Jan 1938: 22.

478. Carson, E.H.A., "Relics of *Dracula*", *The Canadian Bookman* 20 (1938): 62.

Biographical Material and Obituaries

479. A.B. [Pseud.], "Bravo Stoker" [cartoon], *The Entr'acte*, 23 Sept 1882: 9. Commentary on p.3.

480. T.R. [Pseud.], "The Latest Winners of the Royal Humane Society's Medal" [cartoon], *The Penny Illustrated Paper*, 4 Nov 1882: 296.

481. Anon., "Bram Stoker", in *The Green Room Book and Who's Who on the Stage*, London: T. Sealey Clark, 1907.

482. Anon., "Death of Mr Bram Stoker. Sir H. Irving's Manager", *The Daily Telegraph*, 22 April 1912: 6.

483. Anon., "Obituary: Mr Bram Stoker", *The Times*, 22 April 1912: 15.

484. Anon., "Tribute to Bram Stoker", *The New York Times*, 23 April 1912: 12.

485. Anon., "Bram Stoker", in F.M. Colby ed., *The New International Year Book. A Compendium of the World's Progress for the Year 1912*, New York: Dodd, Mead, 1913, p.683.

486. Anon., "Stoker, Abraham, (Biog.) Escritor Irlandés", in *Enciclopedia Vniversal Ilvstrada Evropeo-Americana*, Bilbao: Espasa-Calpe, S.A., 1927, Vol. 57, pp.1201-2.

487. F. Anstey [Pseud., Thomas Anstey Guthrie], *A Long Retrospect*, London and New York: Oxford University Press, 1936, pp.148-9.

488. F. Anstey [Pseud., Thomas Anstey Guthrie], "Bram Stoker Remembered", *The Bram Stoker Society Journal* 2 (1990): 34-5.

489. Belford, Barbara, *Bram Stoker. A Biography of the Author of "Dracula"*, New York: Alfred A. Knopf, 1996.

490. Caine, Hall, "Bram Stoker. The Story of a Great Friendship", *The Daily Telegraph*, 24 April 1912: 16.

491. Farson, Daniel, "Bram Stoker. The Unknown Who Raised Up Dracula", *Cara* 5 (1972): 30-2.

492. Farson, Daniel, *The Man Who Wrote Dracula. A Biography of Bram Stoker*, London: Michael Joseph, 1975.

493. Jackson, Russell, "The Lyceum in Irving's Absence: G.E. Terry's Letters to Bram Stoker", *Nineteenth Century Theater Research* 6 (1978): 25-33.

494. Ludlam, Harry, *A Biography of Dracula. The Life Story of Bram Stoker*, London: Published for The Fireside Press by W. Foulsham, 1962.

495. McIntyre, Dennis, "Literary Figures", *The Meadow of the Bull*, Raheny: Shara, 1987, pp.197-9.

496. McNally, Raymond T., "Stoker, Bram, (1847-1912)", in B. Johnston ed., *Collier's Encyclopedia with Bibliography and Index*, New York: Macmillan Educational, 1989, Vol 21, p.540.

497. Melton, J. Gordon, "Stoker, Abraham 'Bram'", *The Vampire Book. The Encyclopedia of the Undead*, Detroit: Visible Ink, 1994, pp.583-7.

498. Pozzuoli, Alain, *Bram Stoker. Prince des Ténèbres*, Paris: Librairie Séguier, 1989.

499. Shepard, Leslie, "The Library of Bram Stoker", *The Bram Stoker Society Journal* 4 (1992): 28-34.

500. Shepard, Leslie, "A Note on the Death Certificate of Bram Stoker", *The Bram Stoker Society Journal* 4 (1992): 34-6.

501. Shepard, Leslie, "Bram Stoker's Dublin", *The Bram Stoker Society Journal* 5 (1993): 9-13.

502. Shepard, Leslie, *Bram Stoker. Irish Theatre Manager and Author. With information on where to visit the Dublin locations associated with Bram Stoker*, Dublin: Impact, 1994.

503. Sweeting, Charles, "Bram Stoker", in J.P. Cinnamond ed., *University Philosophical Society, Trinity College Dublin, Centenary Review*, Dublin: The Centenary Committee of the University Philosophical Society, 1953, pp.51-3.

504. Adams, Norman, "Bram Stoker", *Leopard* 2 (22 June 1976): 22-3.

505. Aguirre, Manuel, *The Closed Space: Horror Literature and Western Symbolism*, Manchester: Manchester University Press, 1990.

506. Appleby, Robin S., "Dracula and Dora: The Diagnosis and Treatment of Alternative Narratives", *Literature and Psychology* 39 (1993): 16-37.

507. Arata, Stephen D., "The Occidental Tourist: *Dracula* and the Anxiety of Reverse Colonization", *Victorian Studies* 33 (1990): 621-45.

508. Arter, Janice, *Feminist Reflections on Stoker's Heroines*, Chicago: Adams/Count Dracula Fan Club, 1986.

509. Astle, Richard, "Dracula as Totemic Monster: Lacan, Freud, Oedipus and History", *Sub-Stance* 25 (1980): 98-105.

510. Auerbach, Nina, "Magi and Maidens: the Romance of the Victorian Freud", *Critical Inquiry* 8 (1981): 281-300.

511. Auerbach, Nina, *Our Vampires, Ourselves*, Chicago: University of Chicago Press, 1995.

512. Ayles, Daphne, "The Two Worlds of Bram Stoker", *Dublin Magazine* 9 (1971-2): 62-6.

513. Barclay, Glen St.John, *Anatomy of Horror. The Masters of Occult Fiction*, London: Weidenfeld and Nicholson, 1978.

514. Beagle, Donald, "Eliot's *The Waste Land*", *Explicator* 47/3 (1989): 40-1. [Analyses *Dracula* as a source for *The Waste Land*]

515. Bentley, C.F., "The Monster in the Bedroom: Sexual Symbolism in Bram Stoker's Dracula", *Literature and Psychology* 22 (1972): 27-34.

516. Bierman, Joseph S., "The Genesis and Dating of Dracula from Bram Stoker's Working Notes", *Notes and Queries* 222 (1977): 39-41.

517. Bierman, Joseph S., "*Dracula*: Prolonged Childhood Illness and the Oral Triad", *American Imago* 29 (1972): 186-98.

518. Blinderman, Charles S., "Vampurella: Darwin and Count Dracula", *Massachussetts Review* 21 (1980): 411-28.

519. Bonewits, Wanda, "Dracula, the Black Christ", *Gnostica* 4 (1975): 28-9.

520. Boone, Troy, "'He is English and Therefore Adventurous': Politics, Decadence and *Dracula*", *Studies in the Novel* 25 (1993): 76-91.

521. Botting, Fred, "*Dracula*, Romance and the Radcliffean Gothic", *Women's Writing: the Elizabethan to Victorian Period* 1 (1994): 181-201.

522. Botting, Fred, *Gothic*, London: Routledge (The New Critical Idiom), 1996, pp.144-54.

523. Bouët, Jacques, *Dracula, le vovoïde et le vampire*, Paris: Univ. Paul Valéry, 1985.

524. Brederoo, N.J., "*Dracula* in Film", in Valeria Tinkler-Villani and Peter Davidson, eds., *Exhibited by Candlelight: Sources and Developments in the Gothic Tradition*, Amsterdam: Rodopi, 1995, pp.271-81.

525. Brennan, Matthew C., "Repression, Knowledge and saving Souls: The Role of the 'New Woman' in Stoker's *Dracula* and Murnau's *Nosferatu*", *Studies in the Humanities* 19 (1992): 1-10.

526. Broich, Ulrich, "Charakterkonstitution und Modelle für die Erklärung menschlichen Verhaltens im englischen und franzöischen Roman dies 19 jahrhunderts", *Poetica: Zeitschrift für Sprach- und Literaturwissenschaft* 25 (1993): 338-59.

527. Buican, Denis, *Dracula et ses avatars: de Vlad l'Empaleur à Staline et Ceaucescu*, Paris: Espace Europeén, 1991.

528. Byers, Thomas B., "Good Men and Monsters: The Defenses of *Dracula*", *Literature and Psychology* 31 (1981): 24-31.

529. Carlson, M.M., "What Stoker Saw: The History of the Literary Vampire", *Folklore Forum* 10 (1977): 26-32.

530. Carter, Margaret L., *Shadow of a Shade: A Survey of Vampirism in Literature*, New York: Gordon, 1975.

531. Carter, Margaret L., ed., *Dracula. The Vampire and the Critics*, Ann Arbor: U.M.I. Research, 1987.

532. Carter, Margaret L., ed., *The Vampire in Literature. A Critical Bibliography*, Ann Arbor and London: U.M.I. Research, 1989.

533. Casquel, Miguel G., *Drácula: mito y realidad del vampirismo*, Madrid: Maisal, 1979.

534. Case, Alison, "Tasting the Original Apple: Gender and the Struggle for Narrative Authority in *Dracula*", *Narrative* 1 (1993): 223-43.

535. Case, S.E., "Tracking the Vampire", *Differences. A Journal of Feminist Cultural Studies* 3/2 (1991): 1-20.

536. Coats, Daryl R., "Bram Stoker and the Ambiguity of Identity", *Publication of the Mississippi Philological Association* (1984): 88-105.

537. Copjec, J., "Vampires, Breast Feeding and Anxiety", *October* 58 (1991): 25-43.

538. Copper, Basil, *The Vampire in Legend and Fact*, New York: Citadel, 1973.

539. Cornwell, Neil, *The Literary Fantastic from Gothicism to Postmodernism*, Brighton: Harvester Wheatsheaf, 1990.

540. Craft, Christopher, "'Kiss Me with Those Red Lips': Gender and Inversion in Stoker's *Dracula*", *Representations* 8 (1984): 107-33; rpt in Elaine Showalter, ed., *Speaking of Gender*, New York: Routledge, 1989, pp.316-242.

541. Cranny-Francis, Anne, "Sexual Politics and Political Repression in Bram Stoker's *Dracula*", in Clive Bloom, Brian Docherty, Jane Gibb, and Keith Shand, eds., *Nineteenth Century Suspense: From Poe to Conan Doyle*, Basingstoke: Macmillan, 1988, pp.64-79.

542. Croley, Laura Sagolia, "The Rhetoric of Reform in Stoker's *Dracula*: Depravity, Decline and the *Fin de Siècle* 'Residuum'", *Criticism: A Quarterly for Literature and the Arts* 37/1 (1995): 85-108.

543. Cusick, Edmund, "Stoker's Languages of the Supernatural: A Jungian Approach to the Novels", in Victor Sage and Allan Lloyd Smith, eds., *Gothick. Origins and Innovations*, Amsterdam: Rodopi, 1994, pp.140-9.

544. Dalby, Richard, *Bram Stoker: A Bibliography of First Editions*, London: Dracula, 1983.

545. Dalby, Richard, "The Jewel of Seven Stars", in Stephen Jones and Kim Newman, eds., *Horror: 100 Best Books*, London: New English Library/Hodder and Stoughton, 1992, pp.81-5.

546. Daly, Nicholas, "Irish Roots: The Romance of History in Bram Stoker's *The Snake's Pass*", *Literature and History* 4/2 (1995): 42-70.

547. Demetrakopoulos, Stephanie, "Feminism, Sex Role Exchanges, and Other Subliminal Fantasies in Bram Stoker's *Dracula*", *Frontiers: A Journal of Women's Studies* 2 (1977): 104-13

548. Denman, Peter, "LeFanu and Stoker: A Probable Connection", *Éire-Ireland* 9 (1974): 152-8.

549. Dowse, Robert E., and Palmer, David, "*Dracula*. The Book of Blood", *The Listener* 7, March 1963.

550. Drummond, James, "Bram Stoker's Cruden Bay", *The Scots' Magazine*, April 1976: 23-8.

551. Drummond, James, "Dracula's Castle", *The Weekend Scotsman*, 26 June 1976: 1

552. Dukes, Paul, "*Dracula*: Fact, Legend and Fiction", *History Today* 32 (1982): 44-7.

553. Dyer, Richard, "Children of the Night: Vampirism as Homosexuality, Homosexuality as Vampirism" in Susannah Radstone, ed., *Sweet Dreams: Sexuality and Gender in Popular Fiction*, London: Lawrence and Wishart, 1988, pp.47-72.

554. Faig, Kenneth W., "About Bram", *Romantist* 4-5 (1980-1): 39-40.

555. Feimer, Joel N., "Bram Stoker's *Dracula*: The Challenge of the Occult to Science, Reason and Psychiatry" in Michelle Langford, ed., *Contours of the Fantastic: Selected Essays from the Eighth International Conference on the Fantastic in the Arts*, New York: Greenwood, 1994, pp.165-71.

556. Finné, Jacques, *Bibliographie de Dracula*, Lausanne: Editions l'Age d'Homme, 1986.

557. Florescu, Radu, and McNally, Raymond T., *The Complete Dracula*, Acton MA: Copley, 1992.

558. Fontana, Ernest, "Lombroso's Criminal Man and Stoker's Dracula", *Victorian Newsletter* 66 (1984): 25-7.

559. Frayling, Christopher ed., *The Vampyre*, London: Gollancz, 1978.

560. Frayling, Christopher, "Just a Kiss at Bedtime", *Review Guardian*, 14 Nov 1981: 23-4.

561. Frayling, Christopher ed., *Vampyres. Lord Byron to Count Dracula*, London: Faber and Faber, 1991.

562. Fry, Carrol L., "Fictional Conventions and Sexuality in *Dracula*", *Victorian Newsletter* 42 (Fall 1972): 20-2.

563. Gagnier, Regenia, "Evolution and Information, or Eroticism and Everyday Life, in *Dracula* and Late-Victorian Aestheticism", in Regina Barrecca, ed., *Sex and Death in Victorian Literature*, Basingstoke: Macmillan, 1990, pp.140-57.

564. Garnett, Rhys, "*Dracula* and *The Beetle*: Imperial and Sexual Guilt and Fear in Late Victorian Fantasy", in Rhys Garnett, and R.J. Ellis, eds., *Science Fiction Roots and Branches: Contemporary Critical Approaches*, New York: St. Martin's, 1990, pp.30-54.

565. Gattegno, Jean, "Folie, Croyance, et Fantastique dans *Dracula*", *Littérature* 8 (1972): 72-83.

566. Geary, Robert F., "The Powers of Dracula", *Journal of the Fantastic in the Arts* 4 (1991): 81-91.

567. Glover, David, "Bram Stoker and the Crisis of the Liberal Subject", *New Literary History* 23 (1992): 983-1002.

568. Glut, Donald F., *The Dracula Book*, New Jersey: Scarecrow, 1975.

569. Greenway, John L., "Seward's Folly: *Dracula* as a Critique of 'Normal Science'", *Stanford Literature Review* 3 (1986): 213-30.

570. Griffin, Gail B., "'Your Girls That You Love Are Mine': *Dracula* and the Victorian Male Sexual Imagination", *International Journal of Women's Studies* 3 (1980): 454-65.

571. Gutjahr, Paul, "Stoker's *Dracula*", *Explicator* 52/1 (1993): 36-8.

572. Haining, Peter, *The Dracula Centenary Book*, London: Souvenir, 1987; rpt twice as *The Dracula Scrapbook*, London: New English Library, 1976; and London: Chancellor, 1992.

573. Halberstam, Judith, "Technologies of Monstrosity: Bram Stoker's Dracula", *Victorian Studies* 36 (1993): 333-52, rpt in Sally Ledger and Scott McCracken, eds., *Cultural Politics at the Fin de Siècle*, Cambridge: Cambridge University Press, 1995, pp.248-66.

574. Harmening, Dieter, *Der Anfang von Dracula Zur Geschichte von Geschichten*, Würzburg: Königshausen & Neumann, 1983.

575. Hatlen, Burton, "The Return of the Repressed/Oppressed in Bram Stoker's *Dracula*", *Minnesota Review* 15 (1980): 80-97.

576. Havlik, Robert J., "Walt Whitman and Bram Stoker: The Lincoln Connection", *Walt Whitman Review* 4 (1987): 9-16.

577. Hennelly, Mark M., "*Dracula*: The Gnostic Quest and Victorian Wasteland", *English Literature in Transition* 20 (1977): 13-26.

578. Hennelly, Mark M., "Twice-Told Tales of Two Counts: *The Woman in White* and *Dracula*", *The Wilkie Collins Society Journal* 2 (1982): 15-31.

579. Hennelly, Mark M., "The Victorian Book of the Dead: *Dracula*", *Journal of Evolutionary Psychology* 13 (1992): 204-11.

580. Hennelly, Mark M., "The Victorian Book of the Dead: *Dracula*, Part III", *Journal of Evolutionary Psychology* 15 (1993): 1-2.

581. Hollinger, Veronica, "The Vampire and the Alien: Variations on the Outsider", *Science-Fiction Studies* 16 (1989): 145-60.

582. Hood, Gwenyth, "Sauron and Dracula", *Mythlore* 52 (1987): 11-7.

583. Howes, Marjory, "The Mediation of the Feminine: Bisexuality, Homoerotic Desire, and Self-Expression in Bram Stoker's *Dracula*", *Texas Studies in Literature and Language* 30 (1988): 104-19.

584. Hughes, William, "'This Mystifying Medley of Ancient Egypt and the Twentieth Century': Bram Stoker and Popular Egyptology", *The Bram Stoker Society Journal* 4 (1992): 37-45.

585. Hughes, William, "Profane Resurrections: Bram Stoker's Self-Censorship in *The Jewel of Seven Stars*", in Allan Lloyd Smith and Victor Sage, eds., *Gothick: Origins and Innovations*, Amsterdam: Rodopi, 1994, pp.132-9.

586. Hughes, William, "'Militant Instinct': The Perverse Eugenics of Bram Stoker's Fiction", *The Bram Stoker Society Journal* 6 (1994): 11-9.

587. Hughes, William, "'For Ireland's Good': The Reconstruction of Rural Ireland in Bram Stoker's *The Snake's Pass*", *Irish Studies Review* 12 (Autumn 1995): 17-21.

588. Hughes, William, "'So Unlike the Normal Lunatic': Abnormal Psychology in Bram Stoker's *Dracula*", *University of Mississippi Studies in English* New Series 11-2 (1993-5): 1-10.

589. Hyles, Vernon, "Stoker, *Frankenstein*, *Dracula*, Sex, Violence and Incompetence", *Round Table of South Central College English Association* 27 (1986): 7-8.

590. Irvin, Eric, "Dracula's Friends and Forerunners", *Quadrant* 135 (1978): 42-4.

591. Jann, Rosemary, "Saved by Science? The Mixed Messages of Stoker's *Dracula*", *Texas Studies in Literature and Language* 31 (1989): 273-87.

592. Johnson, Alan, "'Dual Life': The Status of Women in Stoker's *Dracula*", *Tennessee Studies in Literature* 27 (1984): 20-39.

593. Johnson, Alan, "Bent and Broken Necks: Signs of Design in Stoker's *Dracula*", *Victorian Newsletter* 72 (1987): 17-24.

594. Keats, Patrick, "Stoker's *Dracula*", *Explicator* 50 (1991): 26-7.

595. Kittler, Friedrich, "Dracula's Legacy", *Stanford Humanities Review* 1 (1989): 143-73.

596. Kline, Salli J., *The Degeneration of Women. Bram Stoker's Dracula as Allegorical Criticism of the Fin de Siècle*. Mit einer Zusammenfassung auf deutsch, Avec un résumé en français, Rheinbach-Merzbach: CMZ-Verlag, 1992.

597. Leatherdale, Clive, *Dracula. The Novel and the Legend. A Study of Bram Stoker's Gothic Masterpiece*, Wellingborough: Aquarian, 1985.

598. Leatherdale, Clive, *Dracula. The Novel and the Legend. A Study of Bram Stoker's Gothic Masterpiece.* "Revised Edition", Brighton: Desert Island, 1993.

599. Leatherdale, Clive, *The Origins of Dracula. The Background to Bram Stoker's Gothic Masterpiece*, London: William Kimber, 1987.

600. Lidston, Robert, "*Dracula* and *'Salem's Lot*: Why the Monsters Won't Die", *West Virginia University Philological Papers* 28 (1982): 70-8.

601. Llopis, Rafael, *Historia natural de los cuentos de miedo*, Madrid: Ediciones Júcar, 1974, pp.169-79.

602. Lottes, Wolfgang, "*Dracula* & Co. Der Vampir in der englischen Literatur", *Archiv für das Studium der Neueren Sprachen und Literaturen* 220 (1983): 285-9.

603. MacFie, Sian, "'They Suck Us Dry': A Study of Late Nineteenth-Century Projections of Vampiric Women", in Philip Shaw, and Peter Stockwell, eds., *Subjectivity and Literature from the Romantics to the Present Day*, London: Pinter, 1991, pp.58-67.

604. MacGillivray, Royce, "*Dracula*: Bram Stoker's Spoiled Masterpiece", *Queen's Quarterly* 79 (1972): 518-27.

605. Marigny, Jean, *Le vampire dans la littérature anglo-saxonne*, Paris: Didier Erudition, 1985.

606. Marocchino, Kathryn, "Structural Complexity in Bram Stoker's *Dracula* — Unravelling the Mysteries", *The Bram Stoker Society Journal* 2 (1990): 3-21.

607. Martin, Philip, "The Vampire in the Looking-Glass: Reflection and Projection in Bram Stoker's *Dracula*", in Clive Bloom, Brian Docherty, Jane Gibb, and Keith Shand, eds., *Nineteenth Century Suspense: From Poe to Conan Doyle*, Basingstoke: Macmillan, 1988, pp.80-92.

608. Mayne, Judith, "*Dracula* in the Twilight: Murnau's *Nosferatu* (1922)" in Eric Rentschler, ed., *German Film and Literature: Adaptations and Transformations*, New York: Methuen, 1986, pp.25-39.

609. McBride, W.T., "Dracula and Mephistopheles — Shyster Vampires", *Literature-Film Quarterly* 18/2 (1990): 116-21.

610.   McDonald, Beth E., "The Vampire as Trickster Figure in Bram Stoker's *Dracula*", *Extrapolation* 33 (1992): 128-44.

611.   McDonald, Jan, "'The Devil is Beautiful': *Dracula* — Freudian Novel and Feminist Drama" in Peter Reynolds, ed., *Novel Images: Literature in Performance*, London: Routledge, 1993, pp.80-104.

612.   McGrath, Patrick, "Suckers for Punishment", *The Sunday Times*, 6 Sept 1992: 8.

613.   McGuire, Karen, "The Artist as Demon in Mary Shelley, Stevenson, Walpole, Stoker and King", *Gothic* [Baton Rouge] 1 (1986): 1-5.

614.   McGuire, Karen, "Of Artists, Vampires and Creativity", *Studies in Weird Fiction* 11 (1994): 2-4.

615.   McNally, Raymond T., and Florescu, Radu, *In Search of Dracula. A True History of Dracula and Vampire Legends*, London: New English Library, 1973.

616.   McWhir, A., "Pollution and Redemption in *Dracula*", *Modern Language Studies* 17 (1987): 31-40

617.   Miller, Elizabeth, "*Dracula*: The Narrative Patchwork", *Udolpho* (Sept 1994): 27-30.

618.   Morrison, Ronald D., "Reading Barthes and Reading *Dracula*: Between Work and Text", *Kentucky Philological Review* 9 (1994): 23-8.

619.   Murphy, Brian, "The Nightmare of the Dark: The Gothic Legacy of Count Dracula", *Odyssey* 1 (1976): 9-15.

620.   Muth, Jon J., *Dracula. Symphonie des Grauens*, ed. Georg F. Tempel, trans. Karlheinz Borchert, [München]: Ehapa, 1993.

621.   Nandris, Grigor, "The History of Dracula. The Theme of His Legend in the Western and Eastern Literatures of Europe", *Comparative Literature Studies* 3 (1966): 367-96.

622.   Nicholson, Mervyn, "Bram Stoker and C.S. Lewis: *Dracula* as a Source for *That Hideous Strength*", *Mythlore: A Journal of J.R.R. Tolkein, C.S. Lewis, Charles Williams, and the Genres of Myth and Fantasy* 19 (1993): 16-22.

623.   Naugrette, Jean-Pierre, "Discours du corps, ordre du discours: De Stevenson à Kafka", in Brugiére, Bernard, ed., *Les Figures du corps dans la*

littérature et la peinture anglaises et americaines de la Renaissance à nos jours, Paris: Pubs. de la Sorbonne, 1991, pp.139-48.

624. O'Brien, Thomas F., "Re: Vampires, Again", *The Baker Street Journal: An Irregular Quarterly of Sherlockiana* 37 (1987): 154-7.

625. Oinas, Felix, "East European Vampires and *Dracula*", *Journal of Popular Culture* 16 (1982): 108-16.

626. Paris, Mark S., "From Clinic to Classroom While Uncovering the Evil Dead in *Dracula*: A Psychoanalytic Pedagogy", in James M. Calahan and David B. Downing, eds., *Practising Theory in Introductory College Literature*, Urbana: National Council of Teachers of English, 1991, pp.47-56.

627. Perrot, Jean, "Bram Stoker, Rudyard Kipling, Oscar Wilde et la Franc-Maconnerie lyrique de l'enfant divin", *Revue des Sciences Humaines* 99 (1992): 183-205.

628. Perry, Dennis R., "Whitman's Influence on Stoker's *Dracula*", *Walt Whitman Quarterly Review* 3 (1986): 29-35.

629. Phillips, Robert, and Rieger, Branimir, "The Agony and the Ecstasy: A Jungian Analysis of Two Vampire Novels, Meredith Ann Pierce's *The Darkangel* and Bram Stoker's *Dracula*", *West Virginia University Philological Papers* 31 (1986): 10-9.

630. Pick, Daniel, "'Terrors of the Night': *Dracula* and 'degeneration' in the late nineteenth century", *Critical Quarterly* 30 (1984): 71-87.

631. Pope, Rebecca A., "Writing and Biting in *Dracula*", *LIT: Literature Interpretation Theory* 1 (1990): 199-216.

632. Power, Albert, "Bram Stoker and the Tradition of Irish Supernatural Literature", *The Bram Stoker Society Journal* 3 (1991): 3-21.

633. Pullinger, Kate, "My Hero. Kate Pullinger on Dracula", *The Independent Magazine*, 24 June 1989: 54

634. Raible, Christopher Gist, "Dracula: Christian Heretic. The themes of the *Dracula* tale are mirror inversions or perversions of Christian truths", *Christian Century* 96 (1979): 103-4.

635. Riccardo, Martin V., *Vampires Unearthed: the Complete Multi-Media Vampire and Dracula Bibliography*, New York: Garland, 1983.

636. Richardson, Maurice, "The Psychoanalysis of Ghost Stories", *The Twentieth Century* 166 (1959): 419-31.

637. Roberts, Bette B., "Victorian Values in the Narration of *Dracula*", *Studies in Weird Fiction* 6 (1989): 10-4.

638. Ronay, Gabriel, *The Truth About Dracula*, New York: Stein and Day, 1972.

639. Roth, Lane, "*Dracula* Meets the Zeitgeist: *Nosferatu* (1922) as Film Adaptation", *Literature-Film Quarterly* 7 (1979): 309-13.

640. Roth, Phyllis A., "Suddenly Sexual Women in Bram Stoker's *Dracula*", *Literature and Psychology* 27 (1977): 113-21.

641. Roth, Phyllis A., *Bram Stoker*, Boston: Twayne, 1982.

642. Rottensteiner, Franz, *The Fantasy Book: An Illustrated History from Dracula to Tolkein*, New York: Collier, 1978.

643. Ryan, J.S., "Perilous Roads to the East, from Weathertop and through the Borgo Pass", *Minas Tirith Evening-Star: Journal of the American Tolkein Society* 17 (1988): 12-4.

644. Sage, Victor, *Horror Fiction in the Protestant Tradition*, Basingstoke: Macmillan, 1988, pp.50-7, pp.176-86,

645. Sage, Victor, "Gothic Laughter: Farce and Horror in Five Texts", in Victor Sage and Allan Lloyd Smith, eds., *Gothick. Origins and Innovations*, Amsterdam: Rodopi, 1994, pp.190-203.

646. Santos, Care, "La paradoja del creador: Bram Stoker", *Quimera: Revista de Literatura* 117 (1993): 12-6.

647. Schaffer, Talia, "'A Wilde Desire Took Me': The Homoerotic History of *Dracula*", *ELH* 61 (1994): 381-425.

648. Schmitt, Cannon, "Mother Dracula: Orientalism, Degeneration, and Anglo-Irish National Subjectivity at the *Fin de Siècle*", *Bucknell Review* 38/1 (1994): 25-43.

649. Schroeder, Aribert, *Vampirismus: Seine Entwicklung vom Thema zum Motiv*, Frankfurt: Akademische Verlagsgesellschaft, 1973.

650. Seed, David, "The Narrative Method of *Dracula*", *Nineteenth Century Fiction* 40 (1985): 61-75

651. Seltzer, Mark, "Serial Killers", *Differences: A Journal of Feminist Cultural Studies* 5 (1993): 92-128.

652. Senf, Carol A., "*Dracula*: The Unseen Face in the Mirror", *Journal of Narrative Technique* 9 (1979): 160-70.

653. Senf, Carol A., "*Dracula*: Stoker's response to the New Woman", *Victorian Studies* 26 (1982): 33-49.

654. Senf, Carol A., "*Brides of Dracula*: From Novel to Film", *Studies in Popular Culture* 7 (1984): 64-71.

655. Senf, Carol A., *The Vampire in Nineteenth-Century English Literature*, Bowling Green, Ohio: Popular, 1988.

656. Senf, Carol A., "*The Lady of the Shroud*: Stoker's Successor to *Dracula*", *Essays in Arts and Sciences* (1990): 82-96.

657. Senf, Carol A., ed., *The Critical Response to Bram Stoker* (Critical Responses in Arts and Letters, number 9), Westport, Connecticut: Greenwood, 1993.

658. Shuster, Seymour, "*Dracula* and Surgically Induced Trauma in Children", *British Journal of Medical Psychology* 46 (1973): 259-70.

659. Siegel, Mark Richard, *Hugo Gernsback, Father of Modern Science Fiction: With Essays on Frank Herbert and Bram Stoker*, San Bernardino, California: Borgo, 1988.

660. Skal, David J., *Hollywood Gothic: The Tangled Web of Dracula from Novel to Stage to Screen*, London: Andre Deutsch, 1992.

661. Smith, Malcolm, "*Dracula* and the Victorian Frame of Mind", *Trivium* 24 (1989): 76-97.

662. Spear, Jeffrey L., "Gender and Sexual Dis-Ease in *Dracula*" in Lloyd Davis ed., *Virginal Sexuality and Textuality in Victorian Literature*, Albany: State University of New York Press, 1993, pp.179-92.

663. Spencer, Kathleen L., "Purity and Danger: *Dracula*, the Urban Gothic and the Late-Victorian Degeneracy Crisis", *ELH* 59 (1992): 197-225.

664. Stade, George, "Dracula's Women", *Partisan Review* 53 (1986): 200-15.

665. Stade, George, "Dracula's Women, and Why Men Love to Hate Them", in Gerald I. Fogel, Frederick M. Lane, and Robert S. Liebert, eds., *The Psychology of Men: New Psychoanalytic Perspectives*, New York: Basic, 1986, pp.25-48.

666. Stein, Gérard, "«Dracula» ou la circulation du «Sans»", *Littérature* 8 (1972): 84-99.

667. Stevenson, John Allen, "A Vampire in the Mirror: The Sexuality of *Dracula*", *PMLA* 103 (1988): 139-49.

668. Stewart, Garrett, "'Count Me In': *Dracula*, Hypnotic Participation, and the Late-Victorian Gothic of Reading", *LIT: Literature Interpretation Theory* 5/1 (1994): 1-18.

669. Temple, Philip, "The Origins of *Dracula*", *The Times Literary Supplement* number 4205 (1983): 1216.

670. Thompson, David, "Supinely Anticipating Red-Eyed Shadows: A Jungian Analysis of Bram Stoker's *Dracula*", *Journal of Evolutionary Psychology* 15 (1994): 289-301.

671. Todd, Janet M., "The Classic Vampire", in Michael Klein and Gillian Parker, eds., *The English Novel and the Movies*, New York: Ungar, 1981, pp.197-210.

672. Tracy, Robert, "Loving You All Ways: Vamps, Vampires, Necrophiles and Necrofilles in Nineteenth-Century Fiction", in Regina Barreca, ed., *Sex and Death in Victorian Literature*, Basingstoke: Macmillan, 1990, pp.32-59.

673. Tremayne, Peter, "The Irish Dracula", *The Bram Stoker Society Journal* 1 (1989): 29-31.

674. Twitchell, James B., "The Vampire Myth", *American Imago* 37 (1980): 83-92.

675. Umland, Samuel J., *Dracula: Notes, Including Life of the Author, General Plot Summary*, Lincoln, Neb.: Cliff's Notes, 1983.

676. Varma, Devandra P., "The Genesis of Dracula: A Re-Visit", in Peter Underwood,ed., *The Vampire's Bedside Companion*, London: Frewin, 1975.

677. Wall, Geoffrey, "'Different from Writing': *Dracula* in 1897", *Literature and History* 10 (1984): 15-23.

678. Waller, Gregory A., *The Living and the Undead: From Stoker's Dracula to Romero's Dawn of the Dead*, Urbana: University of Illinois Press, 1986.

679. Walsh, Thomas P., "*Dracula*: Logos and Myth", *Research Studies* 47 (1979): 229-37.

680. Warwick, Alexandra, "Vampires and the Empire: fears and fictions of the 1890s", in Sally Ledger & Scott McCracken eds., *Cultural Politics at the Fin de Siècle*, Cambridge: Cambridge University Press, 1995, pp.203-20.

681. Wasson, Richard, "The Politics of *Dracula*", *English Literature in Transition* 9 (1966): 24-7.

682. Weissman, Judith, "Women and Vampires: *Dracula* as a Victorian Novel", *Midwest Quarterly* 18 (1970): 392-405.

683. Wicke, Jennifer, "Vampiric Typewriting: *Dracula* and its Media", *ELH* 59 (1992): 467-93.

684. Williams, Anne, "*Dracula*: Si(g)ns of the Fathers", *Texas Studies in Literature and Language* 33 (1991): 445-63.

685. Wilson, Colin, "*Dracula*", in Stephen Jones and Kim Newman, eds., *Horror: 100 Best Books*, London: New English Library/Hodder and Stoughton, 1992, pp.71-4.

686. Wolf, Leonard, *A Dream of Dracula. In Search of the Living Dead*, Boston: Little Brown, 1972.

687. Wood, Robin, "Burying the Undead: The Use and Obsolescence of Count Dracula", *Mosaic* 16 (1983): 175-87.

688. Zanger, Jules, "A Sympathetic Vibration: *Dracula* and the Jews", *ELT* 34 (1991): 33-43.

689. Zeender, Marie Noëlle, "Miroir de l'âme irlandaise: Aspects du fantastique chez LeFanu, chez Wilde et chez Stoker", *Études Irlandaises: Revue Française d'Histoire, Civilisation et Litterature de l'Irelande* 9 (1984): 67-80.

690. Zeender, Marie Noëlle, "L'Erotisme et la mort: Images de la mere dans trois oeuvres de Bram Stoker", in Roger Bozzetto, Max Duperray, and Alain Chareyre-Mejan, eds., *Eros, science fiction, fantastique, Cahiers du CERLI, Actes du XIe colloque du CERLI, Janvier 26-27 1990*, Aix-en-Provence: Université de Provence, 1991, pp.59-70.

691. Anderson, Donald Travis, *The Female Vampire and the Politics of Gender*. MA, University of Alberta, 1992.

692. Ballasteros González, Antonio, *Narciso: mito y dualidad conceptual en la literatura inglesa victoriana*. PhD, Universidad Complutense, Madrid, 1993.

693. Bashant, Wendy Elizabeth, "*The Double Blossom and a Sterile Kiss*": *Androgynous Theory and its Embodiment in the Nineteenth Century*. PhD, University of Rochester, 1989.

694. Burns, Freddie, *Influences and Innovations: Bram Stoker and the Irish Supernatural Tradition*. MA, The Queen's University of Belfast, 1992.

695. Carter, Margaret L., "*Fiend, Spectre, or Delusion?*": *Narrative Doubt and the Supernatural in Gothic Fiction*. PhD, University of California, Irvine, 1986.

696. Case, Alison Austin, *Writing the Female "I": Gender and Narration in the Eighteenth and Nineteenth Century English Novel*. PhD, Cornell University, 1991.

697. Craft, Christopher Charles, *Another Kind of Love: Sodomy, Inversion, and Male Homosexual Desire in English Discourse, 1850-1897*. PhD, University of California, Berkeley, 1989.

698. Drake, Paula Nicole, *Destruction and Defense: Images of Otherness in Selected British Novels*. PhD, University of Massachusetts, 1987.

699. Gardner, Michelle Joanne, *The Vampire in English Literature*. MA, University of Waterloo, 1991.

700. Halberstam, Judith Marion, *Parasites and Perverts: Anti-Semitism and Sexuality in Nineteenth Century Gothic Fiction*. PhD, University of Minnesota, 1991.

701. Hughes, William, *Discourse and Culture in the Fiction of Bram Stoker*. PhD, University of East Anglia, Norwich, 1994.

702. Hurley, Kelly, *The Novel of the Gothic Body: Deviance, Abjection, and Late-Victorian Popular Fiction*. PhD, Stanford University, 1988.

703. King, Maureen Claire, *From Dracula to the "New Evil": The Social and Sexual Politics of Vampire Fiction.* MA, University of Regina, 1993.

704. Ledwon, Lenora P., *Legal Fictions: Constructions of the Female Legal Subject in Nineteenth-Century Law and Literature.* PhD, University of Notre Dame, 1993.

705. McIntosh, A.A.K., *The Business Manager at Irving's Lyceum, "an individual who calls himself Bram Stoker, who seems to occupy some anomalous position between secretary and valet", or the Forefather of Theatre Administrators.* MLitt, University of Glasgow, 1991.

706. Parker, Berlinda Zellner, *The Narcotic Gaze: Ocular Imagery and the Vampire Motif in Christabel, Carmilla, and Dracula.* MA, Florida Atlantic University, 1982.

707. Powell, Bernadette Lucia, *The House Beautiful and its Mapping of Domestic and Colonial Space: A Study of the Domestic Novel at the Turn of the Century.* DPhil, University of Sussex, 1988.

708. Stott, Rebecca, *The Kiss of Death: A Demystification of the Late-Nineteenth Century "Femme Fatale" in the Selected Works of Bram Stoker, Rider Haggard, Joseph Conrad and Thomas Hardy.* DPhil, University of York, 1989.

709. Street, Douglas Oliver, *Bram Stoker's Under the Sunset: An Edition With Introductory, Biographical and Critical Material by Douglas Oliver Street.* PhD, University of Nebraska, 1977.

710. Thornburg, Thomas Ray, *The Quester and the Castle: The Gothic Novel as Myth with Special Reference to Bram Stoker's Dracula.* EdD, Ball State University, 1970.

711. Ward, Kathleen Martha, *"Dear Sir or Madam": The Epistolary Novel in Britain in the Nineteenth Century.* PhD, University of Wisconsin, Madison, 1989.

712. *Dracula*. "With an Introduction and Notes by Maud Ellmann". Oxford: Oxford University Press (The World's Classics), 1996. 389p.

713. Hall, Jasmine Young, "Solicitors Soliciting. The Dangerous Circulations of Professionalism in *Dracula*", in Barbara Harman and Susan Meyer, eds., *The New Nineteenth Century. Feminist Readings of Underread Victorian Fiction*, New York: Garland, 1996.

714. Hughes, William. "'For the Blood is the Life': The Construction of Purity in Bram Stoker's *Dracula*", in Tracey Hill, ed., *Decadence and Danger: Writing, History and the Fin de Siècle*, Bath: Sulis, 1997.

715. Hughes, William, "The Sanguine Economy: Blood and the Circulation of Meaning in *Dracula*", in Dominique Sipière, ed., *Dracula. Insemination, Dissemination*, Amiens: Université de Picardie, 1996, pp.49-64.

716. Pinkerton, Mark, "Why Westenra?", *The Bram Stoker Society Journal* 7 (1995): 12-15.

717. Principe, David D., "Misbegotten, Unbegotten, Forgotten: Vampires and Monsters in the Works of Ugo Tarchetti, Mary Shelley, Bram Stoker and the Gothic Tradition", *Forum Italicum* 29 (1995): 3-25.

718. Smith, Andrew, *Dracula and the Critics*, Sheffield: Pavic, 1996.

719. Soule, Arun,"*Dracula*: Of Shades and Shadows", *Rajasthan University Studies in English* 20 (1988): 77-83.